SOL JUSTITIAE

LAW

Robert B. L. Murphy

First the Political Kingdom

A personal appraisal of the catholic
left in Britain

Brian Wicker

Sheed and Ward. London and Melbourne

First published 1967
Sheed and Ward Ltd, 33 Maiden Lane, London W.C.2, and
Sheed and Ward Pty Ltd, 28 Bourke Street, Melbourne

Standard book number: 7220 0509 1
This book is set in 10 on 12 pt. Times Roman
Made and printed in Great Britain by
Billing & Sons Limited, Guildford and London

Contents

'Seek ye first the kingdom of God' (Matthew 6:33)
'Seek ye first the political kingdom' (Kwame Nkrumah)

Introduction

This book is written in a time of crisis for christianity. The meaning, the relevance, the credibility, the sincerity of belief and practice are all in question. Within this crisis there is one particular consideration that has led me to attempt to present here, in a brief and simple way, the problems and possibilities (as I see them) that face the radical within the catholic tradition today. This is the rise of a movement in the Roman Catholic Church, especially in Britain, that is trying to understand and interpret christianity in political, and socialist, terms. This movement has gained considerable notoriety in recent years, especially since the appearance of the periodical *Slant* and of books associated with it. The '*Slant* group' has gained a certain reputation for liveliness, intellectual energy, and enthusiasm, but it has also been charged with arrogance, intolerance of opposition, indulgence in private academic jargon, and intellectual snobbery.

To some people it seems to be a new, exciting phenomenon, daring in its use of sources, provocative in its views and disrespectful of authority. But if for these reasons it has gained a good many friends, it has probably won more enemies. Many of the latter have been alienated by the tone, rather than by the content, of *Slant* thinking. But recently at any rate the intellectual quality of the adverse criticism has risen, and the significance of the *Slant* group's work can be judged now by the importance of the opposition it has provoked, as well as by the ideas it has itself put forward. It is undoubtedly a power to be reckoned with. For this reason, I have felt for some time that it would be fitting for someone who has been closely associated with the rise of this movement, but who has no party-line to put forward about it, to try to explain to a wider audience some of the presuppositions that lie behind its work, to give some account of its origins and allegiances, and to offer personal criticisms and to suggest future possibilities.

Many members of this movement would think of themselves as belonging to that group who 'can remain Roman Catholics only because they live their christian lives on the fringe of the institutional church and largely ignore it'[1]—or, to put it another way, who see their christian work as deriving from the many informal groups and institutions that really undertake the seminal thinking in the church, and in relation to which it is the official hierarchy that seems peripheral.[2] But this does not mean that for them christianity is merely a private affair, to which questions of doctrine and authority are irrelevant. On the contrary, they are people to whom theological exploration and participa-

[1] The words are those of Charles Davis, at the press conference announcing his decision to leave the church.
[2] See Herbert McCabe OP, *New Blackfriars* XLVIII, 561 (February 1967), 227–8.

tion in communal christian life are essential, and whose outlook is profoundly shaped by the demands that the modern world makes on a christian mind and conscience—and to whom, therefore, the church, especially the Roman Catholic Church, as actually experienced in its official institutional form, is often an alien and even scandalous irrelevancy.

But to experience the official institutional church as an irrelevancy is by no means the same thing as saying that it is expendable. This is a point that cannot be laboured too often, especially in addressing catholics themselves. For there is an inbuilt tendency in the Roman Church, because of its tradition of centralisation and authoritarianism, and its unfortunate associations with repressive political regimes, to equate authority with something like dictatorship. Any catholic who opposes an authoritarian and dictatorial style of organisation in the church is liable to be automatically labelled as subversive of authority. The notion that authority can be exercised in a democracy quite as effectively as in a dictatorship is too little remembered. Opposition to the decisions of authority is often equated with disbelief in authority as such—instead of being what it may well be, an attempt to re-establish genuine authority in face of some kind of usurpation or distortion. It must therefore be reiterated that the 'catholic left', as a group, does not deny, but positively reaffirms, the necessity of an institutional church. Without institutions and empirical structures the notion of the church is simply meaningless—that is a central contention of the whole 'movement'. It is precisely because the institutional church is so important that its structural inadequacy for its task in the contemporary world is such a scandal, and the development of a strategy for changing it so urgent. The catholic left has tried to identify this inadequacy in its various publications. Some of the most obvious examples will be discussed in the final chapter of this book, which is designed to present some of the themes of the continuing debate.

At this point it is perhaps necessary to define more precisely the term *catholic left* as used in this book. The idea that there is a coherent, well-disciplined *party* of the left within the church is one that has been put about by journalists, and by opponents of the catholic left who want people to see it as a dangerous conspiracy against the church. It is very largely false, though a charge of 'clique-ishness' might not be entirely beside the point. But in this book I am referring to the term rather as a set of assumptions, attitudes, and ideas than as a concerted organisation. These ideas are felt, by the catholic left, to hang together and to form a basis for a more or less consistent policy towards the problems that face the church. What these ideas are will, I hope, emerge in the following pages. They are most fully expounded in the pages of *Slant* and in books associated with that periodical—e.g., the 'Slant Manifesto', *Catholics and the Left*. But these ideas are not held in a vacuum. Like the term *left* itself in its political sense, the catholic left in Britain has a history. I have not tried in this book to give more than a bare sketch of the most recent part of that history. Nor have I attempted to examine the connections between the catholic left in Britain and analogous groups and ideas elsewhere, though these connections are becoming increasingly important. Neither have I linked the catholic left to its equivalents (insofar as they exist) in other christian bodies. My purpose is more modest: to offer a personal view of a limited phenomenon which has caught the imagination and interest of catholics in Britain, and to some extent in the USA too, while bewildering them at the same time.

I have said that this book is written at a time of crisis for christianity. But the crisis is not peculiar to christianity. It is a crisis of western civilisation as a whole. It is the problem of how this civilisation is to effect the transition to a new world in which its own values, structures, and achievements will—necessarily—have a quite different, and in many ways much less significant, role than they have had in the past. But this book is also written out of a belief that christianity has a unique capacity for change under such stress, and that this capacity is one that the civilisation itself needs if the transition is not to become tragic beyond all bearable limits. There are elements in the christian heritage that the world cannot do without, and these cannot be wholly secularised, or divorced from their full ecclesial context. That they are still available is due, in a sense, to the very institution that these values now stand in judgement over. In this sense, then, everyone, not only the committed christian, finds himself in a paradoxical state of tension which he has to resolve for himself. It is strictly impossible for a person bred in this civilisation altogether to cut himself off from the church. It is, even now, in his very bones. But how a necessary repudiation of the human corruption is to be reconciled with commitment to the one institution that makes available the meaning of this very repudiation is a question that only the individual can answer for himself.

The significance of the catholic left is that it has tried, within a certain area of discussion, to plot some of the routes that might profitably be followed. It is trying to discover what kinds of load can be carried along them. Few other groups within the catholic tradition have even begun this task. It is therefore of the utmost importance to the future that such work should be understood and carried on. This book will have succeeded if it helps a few people to respond to the challenge that has been laid down. I feel it is important, however, to insist that, although I have at certain points registered my own differences from the views of some of the catholic left writers themselves, I should not wish this book to be regarded as in any sense either a systematic critique or a full assessment. Its purpose is far more modest: to describe, as I see it, the catholic left and its debt to its sources in a way that is intelligible to readers who are not familiar with either, and to offer some comments on it of my own. Inevitably such a work involves over-simplification and selection, and another author might well want to produce something very different even for the same purpose. Neither my defence nor my criticisms are to be regarded as exhaustive. If I have given the reader just a brief illuminating glimpse of a territory that he will want to explore more fully later on, I shall have done all that this book claims to be trying to do. I give some indication, at the end, of places where further work not mentioned in the text may be consulted on topics that are relevant to the catholic left's position.

My thanks are due to Laurence Bright OP, John Coulson, Neil Middleton, and Walter Stein for reading the book in typescript and making very many useful suggestions and improvements. They are, however, in no way thereby committed to my argument or the conclusions I have drawn.

I am grateful to the following for permission to quote from articles on the 'continuing debate' in the final chapter of this book: to Fr Conrad Pepler (temporary editor of *New Blackfriars*), who has kindly allowed me to reproduce large portions of articles that have appeared in *New Blackfriars*, and to the following authors whose articles were first published in that periodical: Michael Dummett, Terry Eagleton, Bernard Bergonzi, Herbert McCabe OP, and Martin Green. I also wish to thank the editor of *The Clergy Review* for permission to reproduce part of an article by Donald Nicholl which appeared there, and to the author for his willingness to allow this. I should also acknowledge that the editor of *Worldview*, monthly journal of the Council for Religion and International Affairs, has permitted me to quote from an article of my own originally written for *Worldview*. (Full details of these articles are given in Chapter 4.) Finally I wish to thank Mrs D. P. Leigh for typing the book, and my children for helping with the index.

1
The origins and sources of the catholic left

1. *Within the church*

One of the difficulties facing any catholic group that tries to do some intellectual work in common is that it soon becomes identified as a 'party', or even a clique, within the church. There is an endemic tendency in a christianity so deeply influenced, even now, by the scholastic ideals of rationalism, system, and precision as the catholic tradition of the west, to pin down every new idea or expression to some defined context within which it can be managed, accommodated, and made to seem respectable. As long as an authority can be quoted in support of it, or a venerable tradition named within which it has a place, practically any kind of idea, whether intelligent or stupid, can be accepted. It is for this reason that the work of such a group as that associated with *Slant* tends to be seen, by those outside its circle, as more unified and definitive than is in fact the case. Therefore the first emphasis that needs to be given to any account of the work of the catholic left is that it is tentative, exploratory, hypothetical. It is primarily concerned with flying kites, testing out hunches against experience, experimenting with unfamiliar conceptual frameworks in an atmosphere of freewheeling discussion and argument. The way this can best be understood is by taking a brief glance at the origins of the 'movement'.

It would be a mistake to trace the catholic left primarily to a stimulus given by the Second Vatican Council to new types of thinking. In fact, one of the most significant things about it is its wariness towards the declared statements of the council. For the council is seen as having been in many ways (despite Pope John's intentions) the apotheosis of the ecclesiasticism that the left is trying to combat. The commentaries of the journalists—on the behind-the-scene intrigues, on the vote-catching and manoeuvrings for position etc. that went on in Rome—revealed that, despite the theological importance of much of the groundwork that was done, the council as it actually displayed itself in its published utterances did not have the will to achieve the great breakthrough that many people had predicted of it. It now appears to many to have been a great *modernising* influence, intent on refurbishing a stale image, through the introduction into a largely unchanged structure of some new terms and some new disciplines. But the effect of these on fundamentals was limited by the established habits of thought, feeling, and organisation which were left unchanged. What the council did do was, perhaps, to show quite clearly that it is not by such cumbersome methods as these that any fundamental changes of an 'inspirational' kind can come about. It helped a multitude of *ad hoc* groups, focussed on particular interests, to recognise that it is upon their own efforts, using whatever means are suitable, that the necessary changes will depend. The catholic left is one such group, or collection of groups.

The immediate sources of catholic left ideas must be located in two main areas, neither of which can be closely identified with the council. The first was the political climate of the post-1956 years: the second was the moral problem of nuclear warfare and nuclear deterrence. These were obviously closely intertwined in fact. But it is one of the peculiarities of modern catholicism that it was not until a great deal of preliminary work had been done, and intellectual lumber had been removed from the scene, that the intimate connection between the two became clearly apparent to those involved in the argument. It could be said that the catholic left was born out of the recognition that there was no possibility of effectively separating the moral from the political problems of the cold war.

The morality of nuclear warfare, and of the policy of massive nuclear retaliation adopted by both Britain and the USA to prevent it, raised questions so large that, even in an age of supine conformity by the church to any governments that declared opposition to communism, they could not wholly be forgotten. It would be grossly flattering to suggest that the official church was responsible for keeping the problems in view, in England or elsewhere. But unofficially a number of catholic groups did manage, even in the most frozen periods of the cold war, to keep them alive. Notable among these was the largely pacifist minority-group called *Pax*, which was founded in the thirties by Eric

Gill and others, and which has always been looked upon kindly by the English dominicans. After 1956 the annual meetings of this body were swollen through the recruitment to *Pax* of a number of intellectuals who had no deep roots in the pacifist movements of the thirties, and few of whom had ever been conscientious objectors, but who were unable to swallow the official line of the church on the applicability of traditional 'just war' theory to the nuclear situation. The support of a number of prominent dominicans, and also of the lonely but much revered jesuit Archbishop Roberts, lent a certain ecclesiastical prestige to a movement that was growing in confidence and beginning to make itself heard in high places.

Pax supporters began to challenge, radically, the whole foundation of the just-war casuistry in its application to the nuclear problem, and to do so with a weight of authority and a rational seriousness that could not be ignored for long. Increasingly the debate, as it was conducted in the correspondence columns of the catholic press, swung in favour of the unilateralists, not on political grounds but simply because of the sheer force of a moral argument. The more the traditional casuistry was deployed in combatting this tide of feeling and thought, the more obvious its inadequacies became. It was shown up as being, by comparison with the unilateralist case, a frivolous and irresponsible evasion of the real problem.

Of course, had it not been for the fact that all this was taking place at a time when the unilateralist case was being more and more accepted in the country generally, the new thinking in the church would have had far less impact. But this was just the significant new feature in the situation. Now at last, instead of reiterating the old vague generalities which have gone under the misleading heading of 'the church's social doctrine', and which have had no bearing on actual British politics, there was a group of catholics, of impressive learning and dialectical skill, challenging the traditional approach of the church to a fundamental socio-political problem not only in the name of the very moral intransigence that the church itself had come to pride itself on, but also in the same tone of voice that was being used on the political left.

The culmination of this debate was the appearance in 1961 of the symposium edited by Walter Stein and entitled *Nuclear Weapons and Christian Conscience*. It can be reasonably said that this book—by no means identifiable as a 'left' book in the political sense—made mincemeat of the 'traditional' case. In practically all the reviews, the criticisms that were made of it by the traditionalists were already dealt with and answered in the book itself. Such was the paucity of the case that could be mustered against it. Of course, this did not mean that the argument was won, or that the Roman Catholic Church in Britain as a whole was now committed to unilateralism. Indeed, the fact that, despite the case that was made, the same old arguments and attitudes remained in force among those who had control of the church's policy in this area was, I think, crucial to the development of the catholic left itself. For what it showed was that, however strong a case may be in purely philosophical and moral terms, it was of little value in swaying policy (and church policy was no exception) unless it could be seen as part of a total strategy for change that could not avoid becoming, at some point, frankly political. This strategy has been the preoccupation of the catholic left ever since.

Nuclear Weapons and Christian Conscience had an additional significance for the development of the catholic left, which was unsought but, in the event, important. It was refused an imprimatur by the official censor, not because he could find anything contrary to catholic faith or morals in it, but because he felt—or someone above him felt—that the publication of such a book was 'inopportune'. The result was, at times, comic—as, for instance, when Archbishop Beck (who did not agree with its conclusions) strongly commended the book as a serious contribution to a crucial christian problem despite the fact that the censor had refused it permission to be published by a catholic firm. But the result was also serious: for here was a blatant example of an instrument designed to protect people from false doctrine being manipulated (unsuccessfully as it happened) for the purpose of preventing free discussion of a thesis that everyone knew to be not only orthodox, but much more authentically christian than the prevailing just-war casuistry beloved of the official theologians. Thus one of the most important nails that have been driven into the coffin of ecclesiastical censorship was hammered home. (Ecclesiastical censorship is not, in fact, a major topic for catholic left discussion: but it is one of the irritating elements in that process of manipulating ideas and preventing free discussion that has characterised the church in recent centuries; and for that reason, it symbolises the intellectual sterility and political deviousness that the catholic left wants to get rid of in the church.)

As I have said, the true importance of the debate in the late fifties and early sixties among catholics on the nuclear warfare issue lies in the fact that it focussed attention sharply and painfully upon something that the church had almost entirely lost sight of: the relation between a society's cultural and political health and the quality of the christian witness that is possible within it. To understand the meaning of this connection was, perhaps, difficult as long as the norm of catholic thought in the socio-political and cultural spheres was taken to be the 'catholic state'. It was only in a situation where, manifestly, the catholic faith was just a minority eccentricity within a far larger and more varied body of opinion that it was possible to understand how profoundly a genuine, and shared, christian moral awareness depended upon an adequate political foundation.

Perhaps it should be mentioned here that, apart from the work of the unilateralists in the debate already described, another important contribution to the rise of the catholic left was the realisation of how disgracefully the official church had behaved under the nazis in Germany. Gordon Zahn's book *German Catholics and Hitler's Wars* (London and New York, 1963) provided the essential facts on which to make a judgement about this; and the kind of judgement that it demanded was clear. It was the lack of any really felt and lived connection between political commitments and moral commitments that enabled the church so easily to betray itself under Hitler. The root of the trouble was that, for catholics who had been exposed only to the concrete attitudes and teachings of the official church, morality seemed (at best) to be more or less a completely private and individualistic affair. It concerned one's duty to one's neighbour—that is to the individuals one happens to know and live among. Politics, on the other hand, concerned abstract matters, on which moral judgements could not be made. Political problems were to be solved by expediency, and governed by national self-interest and prudent calculation, to which no moral—and no specifically christian —considerations were directly relevant.

At worst, the church actually inculcated an attitude of positive political acquiescence towards the nazi regime. It gave an air of intellectual respectability to a barbarous mythology by way of invoking a christian traditional nationalistic and 'folk' thinking that could easily be manipulated to fascist ends. Exceptional individuals, like the martyr Franz Jägerstätter, who thought differently, and tried to do his political duty precisely according to the dictates of his christian conscience, were considered to be religious maniacs or freaks, not worth serious attention. As long as the government did not attack the property or the prestige of the church too blatantly, or undermine the myths on which catholic political attitudes depended,[1] it had to be obeyed, not even reluctantly but energetically. The significance of the tragedy of catholicism under Hitler, for the catholic left, was that it exemplified the disastrous consequences of accepting the dichotomy between christian morality—a private affair—and politics. A very large part of the intellectual work of the catholic left has been devoted to a meditation

[1] For a discussion of this topic, see J. M. Cameron: 'Catholicism and Political Mythology', *The Night Battle*, London 1962, 1–17.

upon, and an attempt to grapple with, this problem and the ways in which it might be solved.[1]

It was the realisation, by catholics engaged in the nuclear debate, that a genuine christian morality could not be effectively asserted except within the framework of a total strategy for change—i.e, a political strategy —that led them towards the Campaign for Nuclear Disarmament, and through this to the 'new left' itself. But before turning to the 'new left' and its significance for catholics, some mention must be made of several other sources for catholic left ideas and attitudes. As I have said already, the catholic left cannot avoid being mainly an intellectual group, in a broad sense of the term. For this reason, it was inevitable that those organisations that were involved in intellectual activity among catholics should be important in helping to publicise catholic left thinking.

The largest and most comprehensive intellectual body among catholics in Britain is the Newman Association, the official body of catholic university graduates. The significance of the Newman Association to the catholic left has been considerable, in two main ways. First of all, while the association is in no sense committed to any particular political or theological 'slant', a good many of the people concerned in catholic left activities were, and are, members of the association. Through its large programme of conferences, lectures, study groups, and informal discussions, as well

[1] A recent work which is highly relevant here is Carl Amery's *Capitulation: an Analysis of Contemporary Catholicism*, London and New York 1967. It is a study of the social and political causes of the catholic failure to withstand Hitler in Germany in the 1930s, and of the consequences of this failure today.

as through its journal, a platform has been created for the discussion of catholic left ideas, and this has given a distinctive relevance and energy to the association. It has also given the catholic left a forum in which it can test its ideas, discover and try to meet intelligent criticism from informed and committed christians, and generally cut its teeth within a circle of people who can at least be expected to know a little (though often not very much) of its idiom and language.

The second importance of the Newman Association is that it is an official arm of the institutional church, consulted by the authorities on numerous questions. Indirectly, therefore, the informal and largely un-planned association of the catholic left with the New-man Association has given the former a route to the ecclesiastical establishment that it might otherwise have never been able to create for itself. Hence it was not killed off in infancy for lack of nourishment by remaining the preserve of a merely eccentric sect. The Newman Association has given the catholic left a sense of the problems and postures of official catholi-cism, and of the ways in which these may be negoti-ated, which has been invaluable to it. Without this, it might have lacked any sense of realism, and probably any fruitful contact with the work and life of other groups whose activities impinged upon its own.

Secondly, mention must be made of a very loosely organised body known as the December Group. This group arose explicitly as a forum for the free discus-sion of catholic left ideas, and has met annually for a weekend in December since 1958. Its suggestive, not to say revolutionary title, is by no means unapt. From the start this was a group which was designed to discuss catholic social and political questions within the conceptual framework of the new left and its organ, the *New Left Review*. Its importance consists largely in the fact that one of its founders—Neil Middleton— was also a director of Sheed and Ward, and was therefore able to give members of the group a chance of appearing in print whenever they produced anything worth publishing. At first such December Group publications were produced as a special series (Owl-books), of which several were produced within a comparatively short period from 1963–64.[1] It is a significant measure of the progress that the catholic left has made since 1964 that this series has been discontinued, and all subsequent catholic left publications have been produced within Sheed and Ward's ordinary list, alongside works of 'pure' theology and of a more traditional catholic kind.

The December Group has done more than produce a few useful books, however: it has kept alive and nourished a style of thought that is fundamental to the catholic left. By its sheer looseness of organisation and membership it has brought into its orbit new recruits from a variety of views. In fact, it could well be regarded as the principal source of the catholic left as it now exists, and at the present time cannot be distinguished from it.

[1] These were: James D. Halloran, *Control or Consent? A Study of the Challenge of Mass Communication* (1963); Mannes Tidmarsh OP, J. D. Halloran, and K. J. Connolly, *Capital Punishment: a Case for Abolition* (1963); my own *Culture and Liturgy* (1963); and Stanley Windass, *Christianity versus Violence: a Social and Historical Study of War and Christianity* (1964). An American study of the Cuban crisis— Leslie Dewart's *Cuba, Church and Crisis*—was also published in the same series.

The other obvious source of the catholic left is the *Slant* group itself. *Slant* began in Cambridge as an undergraduate magazine, founded by catholic members of the university, mostly drawn from the English faculty, and heavily influenced in their work by Raymond Williams, who was already teaching there. They were members of a new generation of working-class catholic university students, who had been through the catholic education process but who had found its style and content stultifying. They sought to revivify their catholic life, and perhaps the catholic life of the university too, by bringing it into contact with the ideas they had received from a source wholly beyond the confines of the church they knew. The nullity and stuffiness of official catholicism was repugnant to them: but, unlike most of those whose experience was similar to theirs, instead of simply giving up christianity altogether they decided to work within the church for the changes that they felt were needed. *Slant* was the chosen vehicle for this attempt.

The tone of *Slant* at the outset was uncertain, veering rapidly (and to many readers, shockingly) from heavyweight seriousness and intellectualism to flippancy, wit, and even scurrility. (This was the time of the birth of *That Was The Week That Was* and the satire craze.) But this was hardly surprising, considering not only the manner of its birth but the unprecedented nature of its objectives (at least within catholicism in England). But the history of *Slant*—brief though it is—is the history of the subject this book is designed to deal with, so no more needs to be said about it at the present stage.

2. The political 'new left'

The connections between the politics of the catholic left and that of the secular new left have been so intimate, at any rate in terms of ideas, as to be at times practically inextricable. The history and development of the new left, and more particularly of the *New Left Review* and its predecessors, *New Reasoner* and *Universities and Left Review*, is therefore a part of the history of the catholic left itself.

The new left began in the fusion of various left-wing socialist groups at the time of the Suez and Hungary crises in 1956. Its impetus came from a double disillusionment and shock. First, the Hungarian revolt was put down brutally by the very power that had, only recently, begun to admit the enormities, and to try to repair some of the damage, of stalinism in Russia. This led to a widespread abandonment, by socialists, of their traditional loyalty to the Soviet Union and its international role in the creation of socialism. Secondly, and simultaneously, however, the British government showed itself, in the Suez affair, still gripped by the grandiose ambitions of the past, and by the ideology of imperialism that underlay it. If the first event shattered any uncritical support for the Russian way to socialism, Suez shattered the hopes of post-1945 socialist thinkers in the possibility of contemporary British society being able, by a process of inevitable conflict-free evolution, to proceed towards a socialist society in calm and peace.

Hence there began a process of mutual discussion among a very disparate group of intellectuals designed to put forward a criticism of contemporary British society that would be adequate to the realities that had been revealed, and would be radically socialist while at the same time being conspicuously anti-totalitarian and humane in its concern for people, in their total context of life. For some, this still seems to have meant some kind of proletarian revolution, though it was never clear of what kind it would be or when it would come about. For others, the emphasis was rather upon the length, complexity, and subtlety of the political analysis that had to be made, and accepted, before any realistic hope of socialism could be recreated. For this was a time of disillusion and defeat for all who believed in the possibility of a radical political solution to the pressing problems of the world. For most people hope was placed rather in technical innovation, the economic control and manipulation of resources, and the elimination of class-consciousness through affluence. These were to do the job that politics could no longer expect to undertake successfully. But for the new left this implicit fragmentation of the political problem into essentially separate areas, each under the management of specialists who lacked any overall conception of the strategy required, or the problems of power that had to be faced, spelt disaster. It constituted an evasion of what was most urgently needed: namely, a comprehensive, integrated vision of what a humane society would involve, and what kind of philosophy of man and his basic predicament this entailed. The following account of the aims of the new left makes the point usefully (and its tone of voice is characteristic as well):

Its initial ambition . . . was 'to take socialism at full

stretch', applying its values to 'the total scale of man's activities'. This amounted, in effect, to a call for a new and comprehensive theoretical synthesis, capable of mobilizing the full resources of contemporary socialist thought throughout the world—a synthesis of a kind which has never existed on the British Left. It is arguable that only a major structural shock to our society could eventually produce it. This was clearly absent in 1956–57. However, a slow and long-run change in the nature of British society was becoming visible in these years, which created its own characteristic consciousness. British capitalism had, under great pressure, learnt to satisfy certain fundamental human needs: it had achieved a marked reduction in primary poverty [i.e, poverty due to an absolute lack of resources, as distinct from poverty due to maldistribution of resources], a considerable stability of employment, an extensive welfare network. Yet it remained a potentially intolerable and suffocating system even [for], or precisely for, groups in the population which enjoyed a relatively high standard of living. The very satisfaction of traditional needs in turn created new ones, which neo-capitalism refused and thwarted as traditional capitalism had done earlier ones. As material deprivation to a certain degree receded, cultural loss and devastation became more and more evident and important. The chaos and desolation of the urban environment, the sterility and formalism of education, the saturation of space and matter with advertising, the atomization of local life, the concentration of control of the means of communication and the degradation of their content, these were what became the distinctive preoccupations of the New Left.[1]

[1] Perry Anderson, 'The Left in the Fifties', *New Left Review* 29 (January–February 1965), 14–15. The phrases quoted at the beginning are from *Universities and Left Review* 1 (Spring 1957), one of the journals that preceded the present *New Left Review*. It should perhaps be said here that the

If it weren't for the work done by the new left in close discussion and analysis of the social defects indicated towards the end of that passage, this kind of abstract rhetoric would mean little. But the potentially condescending implications of Anderson's tone, in speaking of a universal 'cultural loss and devastation', become less damaging when the work of Richard Hoggart (*The Uses of Literacy*), Stuart Hall and Paddy Whannel (*The Popular Arts*), and Raymond Williams (*The Long Revolution*) are seen as backing it up with fact, intelligent argument, and hard evidence, and when the Pilkington Report is understood as one of the major achievements of the new left's critique of our culture. Similarly, that the 'sterility and formalism of education' has become a widely accepted fact is partly due to the influence of work done by the new left, not only in making a case for comprehensive education, but more subtly in analysing the quality of actual classroom experience and in making a general educational critique out of the specialist work of such researchers as Basil Bernstein, J. W. Douglas, Jean Floud, and others. The question of the control of the mass media became, of course, crucial at the time of Pilkington. (It has again arisen over the prosecution of the pirate radio stations and the government's plans for local broadcasting.) It is not an exaggeration to suggest that a major part of the credit for the partial defeat of the commercial television and radio lobbies, and the pre-

thinking underlying Anderson's critique in the above passage owes much to the early Marx's concept of individual 'alienation' under any form of class-divided capitalist society, and hardly makes sense without it. It should therefore be considered in the light of Marx's influence on the new left in general. See further pp. 30ff. below.

servation of the principle of public-service broadcasting, should go to the new left, for the persistence and the cogency with which their case was presented.

What turned the new left from being merely an intellectual ginger-group into a genuine political movement, however, was its close connection with the Campaign for Nuclear Disarmament (CND). This campaign began as, and to some extent still is, an expression of *moral* disgust at, and rejection of, the nuclear deterrent policy of Britain and the USA. But the new left was largely responsible for giving the campaign what influence it had, by forcing it to recognise that unilateralism could not remain a purely moral protest. The deterrent strategy had to be linked to, and to be understood as arising out of, a political situation and a particular interpretation of that situation that needed to be challenged and overthrown. It was only when CND began to link its demands for nuclear disarmament with a coherent international and defence policy, based upon an interpretation of events different from the one that was currently being offered—i.e, an alternative to the cold-war ideology that was already obsolete— that it started to attract to its ranks large numbers of converts. It then became, for a couple of years (from roughly 1959 to 1961), the most significant political force in Britain, attracting to itself the most energetic and generous spirits in political life. The crown of its achievement was, of course, the famous victory, at the Labour Party's annual conference at Scarborough, of the unilateralist motion on defence policy. However, this was a shortlived triumph. The late Hugh Gaitskell immediately made it clear that he was not going to follow it up in the parliamentary party or anywhere else. Thence from 1961 onwards, the new left was shorn of much of its political influence, CND became dispirited and fragmented, and the new chromium-plated technical slogans of the Wilson era began to take the place of the older socialist arguments within the Labour Party.

Under the influence of the new political facts of the sixties—the collapse of the cold war and of the two-bloc interpretation of international politics, the rise of China as a rival communist power, the Cuban crisis, the replacement of Kennedy by Johnson in the White House and of Khruschev by Kosygin in the Kremlin, and the growing impatience of the 'third world' with western rivalries and colonialist solutions—it was widely predicted that the new left would collapse as a politically significant force. To some extent this has happened. The new left is no longer a force that the Labour Party have to reckon with on every front. But this is partly due to the fact that, under a labour government (especially one with a minute parliamentary majority as the 1964 election produced), genuine socialist criticism is bound to be difficult and embarrassing. Furthermore, there are signs now that, unless the Vietnam conflict is soon resolved, a new tide of politico-moral protest may sweep into the political arena, despite the existence of a labour government, thus recharging all the batteries that CND once kept fully operational. Such a movement would, in fact, be merely a new phase of the CND phenomenon: and if it were to come into the forefront of politics again the same combination of moral protest and political interpretation and strategy would still be required to make it effective.

But in any case, the new left has not wholly disappeared, and the *New Left Review* still carries on the work that it began in the fifties. An understanding of the changes that have taken place in its outlook and philosophy, especially since 1962, is essential to an appreciation of the catholic left. For the catholic left, as a significant group, had hardly appeared during the heyday of CND. Admittedly that *was* the time when catholic unilateralism was at its most energetic, and it was then that the work that led to the publication of *Nuclear Weapons and Christian Conscience* was being done. But, as I have said, this work predated the catholic left as a distinctive force. My own *Culture and Liturgy*, which was perhaps the first book devoted to arguing the case for a catholic left, did not appear until May 1963. *Slant* itself did not appear until the spring of 1964, when CND was at a low ebb, and most of its supporters were actively engaged in trying to help Harold Wilson to power. The catholic left's debt to the new left is therefore, in large measure, a debt to the new left as it has existed since the decline of the latter's political influence, and the consequent rise of a new style and a new objective. This objective seems now to be to suggest a long-term theoretical and critical interpretation of British society, in the context of the whole world-political order of the post-colonial, post-stalinist, and post-nuclear era. This interpretation may (it is felt) offer the theoretical foundation for a new attack on the barriers to socialism when the opportunity comes —an interpretation given in the name of a fully humanist, and humane, philosophy.

In a sense, of course, this was always the aim of the new left. But as both the present editor of the *New Left*

Review (Perry Anderson) and an earlier critic of the movement (Professor J. M. Cameron) agree, there were serious obstacles in the way of achieving it under the original conditions. According to Cameron, the principal obstacles were, first of all, an inadequate philosophical basis. The new left lacked a conception of man and his nature. Secondly, there was a tendency to harbour long-obsolete dreams (obsolete in the British context) of a revolutionary transition to socialism—a 'vestigial bolshevism'. This 'vestigial bolshevism' in the new left was connected (according to Cameron) with the remnants of its allegiance to the Communist Party and to marxist–leninist orthodoxy, conceived as a master science which possessed all the answers to man's most profound questions.[1] These obstacles were regrettable, because the criticisms levelled by new left thinkers against the cultural life of modern Britain were, in themselves, convincing and important, largely because, unlike the vestigial bolshevism, they rested upon a firm empirical foundation, within British history itself. Raymond Williams's *Culture and Society*—the most widely acclaimed, praised, and discussed of all new left books—was the living embodiment of the truth of this assessment. Thus, when Williams recognised that socialists who 'try to prescribe the new man' are, just like conservatives, liable to *force* old images into a new situation and distort and dehumanise man himself in the process, Cameron said that an authentically humane voice is being raised that we must attend to carefully.

A comparison between Cameron's assessment of the

[1] J. M. Cameron, 'The New Left in Britain', *The Night Battle*, 50–75.

problems of the new left, made in 1961, and that of Perry Anderson in 1965, will perhaps reveal the difference of emphasis that has overtaken the new left during the intervening years. For Cameron, a marxist interpretation of man's predicament must, in the ordinary usage of the term, mean an interpretation in the mechanistic tradition of the familiar marxist textbooks. It would be almost paradoxical to claim a marxist allegiance when (as in the case of Alastair MacIntyre) one 'is a kind of protestant marxist who dates the corruption of the faith from the apostolic age itself'.[1] To select only Marx himself—or even only small, and early, portions of his total achievement— and to discard, as almost wholly mistaken, the work of Engels, Lenin, and Stalin, is to be an extremely a-typical and idiosyncratic marxist. The point that is being made here is not just one of terminology— whether it is appropriate to *call* such a selective 'marxist' a marxist at all. It is that, if one is to allow Marx as only one intellectual influence among many others, then the question arises why should one not include, in addition to the thinkers that new left writers have readily allowed into their reference libraries (Freud, Sartre, Lukacs), others who have also contributed notably to the discussion of man's predicament (Buber? Niebuhr? Teilhard?) What, it may be asked, is it that leads the new left to permit the first group, but to exclude the second, as serious influences to be reckoned with?

The answer lies in the philosophical roots of the 'socialist humanism' that the new left proclaims. In that perspective, such a selective marxism seems to be

[1] J. M. Cameron, 'The New Left in Britain', 72.

normal and unidiosyncratic. As an article in a comparatively recent *New Left Review* puts it:

We believe in the usefulness for sociological theory of certain Marxian categories as well as of insights drawn from the phenomenological analysis of social life. This does not imply any doctrinaire commitment. It is important, rather, to show how sociological theory can be enriched by streams of thought coming from outside the sociological tradition in the narrower sense.[1]

But, if it now seems natural, in the climate of the mid-sixties, to draw Marx out of the context of marxism and simply to take him as a useful source for the intellectual analysis of a problem, this very habit—if taken as symptomatic—witnesses to a commitment that has lost its political edge. What was useful and relevant about the analyses of culture, education, the mass media, and the rest, made in the early days of the new left, was that they were always liable, in the context of the period and its possibilities, to issue in practical political actions. They offered a strategy for change that could be adopted in a foreseeable future. The link between the new left's cultural work and the Pilkington Report, between its educational work and the policies of the government on comprehensive schools, between the work on the mass media and the containment of the powerful lobbies for commercial radio and

---

[1] Peter Berger and Stanley Pullberg, 'Reification and the Sociological Critique of Consciousness', *New Left Review* 35 (January–February 1966), 57. It should, however, be noted that some recent writers in *New Left Review* accept the criticism of new left marxism as too selective, and are trying to reinstate the full, authentic achievement of Marx's mature work.

television, between the critique of popular culture and the struggle against an insidious creeping acceptance of a commercialised and hence degutted mass-art, was always evident, even when it was not actually operative.

The price of having the greater theoretical brilliance and élan of the *New Left Review* today is that its ideas seem incapable of political realisation in any foreseeable future. And as this becomes more and more evident to new left writers themselves, so their rhetoric becomes overstrained and abstract. For example, Anderson now recognises the need for what Cameron saw as necessary but absent in the new left of the earlier phase: 'philosophical anthropology, that is, a total theory of man'.[1] But for such a theory to be of any value, he says, it must operate at many levels—it must be able to sustain the most intractable scholarly research, but also to inspire great masses of people by its simplicity. Only marxism, he says, can do this today. It alone can deal, not only with the traditional problems of politics—such things as income distribution and social welfare—but also with the new areas that have now to be grasped in a total political context: that is to say, such problems as the quality and use of cultural resources, the meaning that work in an industrial society can have for the individual, and even the understanding of such social evils as sexual perversion and even madness. (These now have to be understood not as defects of an individual organism, or 'illnesses', but as defects of human relationships

---

[1] Perry Anderson, 'Problems of Socialist Strategy', *Towards Socialism*, ed. Perry Anderson and Robin Blackburn, London 1965, 287.

and of the social structures that shape and influence them.) As Anderson has said:

The traditional conception of socialist politics in the West involved a certain compartmentalized vision of man. It was believed that the whole purpose of politics was to ameliorate the conditions of social existence—to ensure that every member of society had enough money, leisure, shelter and protection to lead the life he wanted. This was, in the traditional view, the liberation of man. We know now how inadequate this view is. Men are not liberated by wage packets or health clinics, although these are indeed indispensable elements in any social liberation. For they are not free in their *activity*, in their *use* of their time. Social-democratic politics rested on the idea that there was an absolute distinction between the communal conditions of existence and the private pursuit of happiness: 'society' and the 'individual'. The truth is that no such clear distinction can be drawn.[1]

It follows, Anderson continues, that

. . . there is ultimately no neutral area, into which the individual can withdraw from society: he is socially at stake in the whole plenitude of his life, in his work, in his art, in his sexuality. In a capitalist society, all these domains of living tend to be confiscated and denied . . . the ultimate goal is, therefore, necessarily, a new model of civilisation, with its own values, its own relations, its own creativity. Socialism is a promulgation of human freedom across the entire existential space of the world.

Unfortunately the force and impressive eloquence of this kind of writing depends very largely on its lack of precision. Anderson recognises this, of course, and

[1] Anderson, 'Problems of Socialist Strategy', 288.

insists that modern socialists are like the German intellectuals of the 1840s: their rarefied criticism is divorced from the political struggle. So 'the task now is to join the two, developing and enlarging theory in the light of a new practice'. But what, in detail, the reader is expected to do, even here, is quite uncertain. In fact, all the weight of the argument is finally placed, when the thread is followed through to its conclusion, on something outside any circles where the European socialist can have direct influence (unless he moves beyond Europe itself into the countries of the developing 'third world'). Anderson insists that affluence and mastery of primary poverty will not eliminate political thought or passion in Europe. How they will affect the details of the commitments I am to make, as a socialist, to the development of British socialism is still unclear. What *is* felt to be clear, however, is the creative character of the revolutions going on in the 'third world'. Our first commitment is finally to remain in contact with these, and not to allow ourselves to be bemused, by the obsolete images of our own colonial past, into thinking of them merely as dangers to our standards or ways of life, or as 'brushfires' to put out by the use of our traditional armed force.

The fundamental uncertainty about immediate political policies that much new left writing exhibits is one of the characteristic elements in the new left that has been carried over into the thinking of the catholic left. This fact—to be examined at length later on—is obviously linked with the increasingly theoretical character of new left writing in recent years, under the pressures that have already been described. But it would be a grave mistake to think that, because the work has been at such a high level of theory, it has no value in the long run. On the contrary, I think that it is of very great importance, and it is necessary to understand in what its importance consists. But to do this will entail some discussion of the philosophical basis of recent new left thinking, and of the way it has been absorbed into the work of the catholic left, and why it has seemed so relevant to people principally concerned to work out a coherent theory of man within a christian, rather than a secular, framework. That task I must leave to the next chapter.

2
The philosophical basis of the catholic left

We have seen that the principal task of the new left today, as expressed by one of its main spokesmen, is to work out a theory of man. It has accepted this as its task because, under present conditions, the possibility of working out specific policies, on particular issues, which would be relevant to the immediate difficulties of our time and which would also be clearly and unambiguously socialist, is extremely difficult. The purpose behind this concentration on theory, then, is to prepare an operational base from which, it is hoped, it will be possible to venture out later into the field of practical policy-formation while maintaining a secure grasp of the fundamental concepts that are necessary. Now it might well be asked at this point why, if that is all the new left is trying to do—and, in any case, it is not all it is doing, though it is the most characteristic occupation—must it entail a socialist, or even leftish, emphasis at all? Is this not something that any politically conscious person would want to do, whether as a conservative or as a liberal or as a socialist? The answer to this question can only be given fully I suppose in the process of actually trying to do the job. The social-ist would say that, as soon as you sincerely and intel-ligently face the difficulties of this task, you begin to see that it is only in a socialist direction that any com-plete answer can be found. But I think that, despite this claim, which can only be verified in experience, there are two points that can be made at the outset.

The first point is that the very notion that a person adopts of the scope and nature of politics will be shaped by an already accepted political position. There is no retreat into a purely private world, as Perry An-derson points out, no 'ultimately neutral area into which the individual can withdraw from society: he is socially at stake in the whole plenitude of his life'. A man's definition of politics, then, is itself a sign of a certain political commitment. The *Slant Manifesto* puts this point well:

By talking about politics we are talking about what it means to be a man, to be alive. All our experience is in this sense political; it has some relation to other men, to social reality . . .

There may be an objection that this is an unfair use of the word 'politics'—that we are weighting our case by giving it an inflated significance. The objection is under-standable if we look at the way the term has been nar-rowed to mean merely the techniques of government, the detailed business of getting and preserving power. Politics has become a matter for the public world—the world be-yond our private, intimate experience—and the relation between our closest values and beliefs, and the imper-sonal world of political manoeuvring has become increas-ingly difficult to make. The temptation is therefore to reject politics altogether as a specialised pursuit of the ambitious, and this is substantially what has happened in most Western societies today. 'It's all politics', 'politics is dirty', 'I'm not politically-minded' are phrases which have become part of our conventional wisdom. This kind of mental barrier can be best got over by seeing that this attitude is itself a deeply political one; if politics is reduced from a matter of ideology and human belief to a specialist profession, the reduction will benefit those who wish to keep their own, dominant, ideology from being questioned. When a Liberal or Labour or Conservative MP says that public ownership is a matter of efficiency (or inefficiency), not a 'doctrine', he is making this kind of reduction.[1]

Of course, it is easy to reply to this by making the same point the other way round. If you make the definition of politics too wide perhaps you are also opting out into a false, private world—i.e, a world in which a few intellectuals can satisfy their personal desire for philosophical speculation by playing with political abstractions that have no immediate bearing on the work of the practical politicians. Thus a too comprehensive definition of politics, too, can be used to justify a certain withdrawal from society. All this must be admitted; and the test of a political philosophy must, in the end, lie in seeing what is made of it in actual political behaviour. But the important point that I am stressing here is that the 'narrow' definition of politics largely adopted in our kind of society today inevitably reflects a reluctance to change the basic structures of that society. In this sense, then, the adoption of a comprehensive definition of politics is, in itself, an assertion of a need for political change of a fundamental kind.

[1] Adrian Cunningham and Terry Eagleton, 'Politics', *Catholics and the Left*, London 1966, 4–5.

Admittedly, it could, taken in itself, be used to justify a change in the direction of fascism as easily as in the direction of socialism. But at any rate it is anti-conservative, and even anti-liberal, if by liberalism is meant, among other things, the valuation of private, personal relations above public, impersonal ones.[1]

What prevents the new left's comprehensive definition of politics from being allowed to drift in a fascist direction is the selection it makes from its philosophical sources. These are very various, and occasionally eccentric—though none the worse for that. But, at any rate as far as the work of the *New Left Review* hitherto is concerned, two stand out as predominant: the early Marx[2], and Sartre. (Substantially similar views are arrived at by Raymond Williams in *The Long Revolution* by the use of a very different, and apparently more homespun and personal, philosophy.) In both cases the socialist impetus is fundamental, springing from an insight which is unmistakably leftward in its orientation.

In order to present this commitment in a simple and intelligible form—at the expense, it must be insisted, of over-simplification—I shall confine my discussion to a few main points that seem to me to be central to

[1] i.e, the kind of liberalism represented by E. M. Forster: 'Personal relations are despised today. They are regarded as bourgeois luxuries, as products of a time of fair weather which is now past, and we are urged to get rid of them, and to dedicate ourselves to some movement or cause instead. I hate the idea of causes . . .' (*Two Cheers for Democracy*, Part 2: 'What I Believe'.)

[2] It should be said, however, that recently an attempt has been made to reintegrate the early Marx's hegelian philosophical and moral critique of capitalism with his later, more technically sophisticated critique. See, for example, Louis Althusser, 'Contradiction and Over-determination', *New Left Review* 41 (January–February 1967), 15–35.

the theory of man and of his modern predicament that the new left has been trying (not of course alone) to work out.

1. Naturalism and socialist humanism

A characteristic slogan of the new left is that it stands for a fully socialist humanism. By this is meant more than just an interpretation of man which is confined to the human realm, excluding all religious perspectives. It also means an interpretation which respects all the fundamental freedoms that man requires for the living of a full and satisfactory life. It is hence frankly anti-totalitarian, and rejects any philosophy that necessarily leads towards the diminution of human needs and aspiration under the pressures of scientific, technical, military, or other anti-humane advances. Of course it denies the validity of the contemporary conservative defence of capitalism, on the grounds that this is, in effect, an endorsement of motivations that are basically inhuman and life-denying. (These motivations are, notably, the elevation of the private profit-motive to pre-eminence in economic thinking, and the acceptance of a society modelled on the idea of a market in which not only things, but people and their freedoms, are thought of as objects for sale.) But it equally firmly rejects the philosophy of official marxist–leninist orthodoxy for similar reasons.[1] For such a

[1] By this orthodoxy I do not mean the works of Marx or Lenin themselves, but rather the codification of these into official 'textbooks' of communist thinking in the USSR, especially under stalinist influence. The distortion of Marx and Lenin into a species of sacred scripture, inspired and inerrant, is no part of the new left concept of a marxist socialism. Socialism is not a secular substitute for christianity. It is

marxism turns men and their deepest interests into purely economic objects. It makes people into collections of material things related by extrinsic and mechanistic forces. But this official orthodoxy is also attacked for another reason. It is seen as a betrayal of Marx's own work, which was dedicated—especially in the earlier phases of his career—to understanding the mechanism which leads capitalism to dehumanise and enslave persons, by treating human persons as if they were objects. Marx tried to show how this process was only temporary, and could be overcome by a deeper understanding of man and his social setting.

The starting point for this socialist humanism is the recognition that the study of man and the study of the rest of the material world require what may be called different *conceptual frameworks*. The great mistake of both marxist–leninist orthodoxy and of the prevalent scientific-humanist tradition that has grown up in the western social-democracies is that they both tend to describe man in the same kind of terms that they use to describe things. Man has been held first of all to be merely a part of nature, open to just the same kind of investigation as other natural phenomena. Of course, there is nothing new in rejecting this assimilation of humanity to purely natural terms. What is distinctive in the socialist-humanism position is the use made, in the framing of an adequate alternative to these philosophies, of ideas drawn from Marx and of modern existentialism.

In the past, philosophical opposition to both marx-

a humanism which—so the catholic left hold—can be deepened and enriched by a christian understanding without being radically displaced in its own secular field.

ist–leninist orthodoxy aand to scientific humanism of the western kind has come principally from traditional religious, or quasi-religious, sources. It has usually taken the form of accepting scientific humanism at its own valuation as a valid way of dealing with nature— including, of course, man insofar as he is a part of nature—but of denying that man is *wholly* a natural object. There is a residual part of him—the spiritual, intellectual, moral, artistic part—which cannot be treated in these terms. For this part of man's life and activity, it has been felt, other concepts are necessary.[1]

Thus, the two conceptual frameworks have hitherto been differentiated by creating a dividing line between two studies of man: the naturalistic, scientific study of him, and the study of those aspects of his life that transcend scientific investigation. The new socialist humanism tries to show that what is wrong with this position is that the dividing line has been wrongly located. It is not between different aspects of human existence, but rather between the human world as a whole and the whole natural world. Furthermore, such humanism insists that the human sciences are prior to, and give meaning to, the natural sciences, not the other way round. For the world of nature, the material world purely 'as it is', conceived of without any dis-

[1] It is worth noting, however, that creative writers of the last one hundred and fifty years or so have often understood things in a more profound way than the philosophers and theologians. Thus, it is highly significant that, from Dickens onwards, there has been a strong tradition in the novel and the drama to understand man's ultimate 'sin' as that of re-ducing whole persons to mere things, not in terms of a failure to maintain the superiority of the 'spiritual' over the 'material' element in human life. See my *Culture and Theology*, London 1966, chapter 3 for a discussion of this topic.

torting human presence or interpretation, is not a reality set over against man's spiritual and moral life. It is simply an abstraction made by man himself. 'Nature' in this sense—the sense the 'natural' scientist has in mind during his working hours—is a product of human thought and activity, and has only as much objective reality as human thought and activity can give it. It is a reality only insofar as it is investigated, described, measured by man. Thus, when the scientist thinks of man simply as a phenomenon in the natural world—say, as an animal subject to the laws of biological evolution—he needs to remember all the time that this way of thinking is one that he has *chosen* to adopt for certain purposes. This choice is what gives rise to the concept of man as a natural phenomenon. In this sense, man the animal is not prior to, and more easily intelligible than, man the mysteriously free, morally responsible person (as scientific humanism tends to suggest). Only a being who is already a full person can think of himself as being in some respects just a kind of animal, an object in the natural world.

What kind of relevance has all this to a humanism that is socialist, or even politically committed in any sense? In order to understand the way such a theoretical framework may have significant political repercussions, in the sense of forcing us to see a practical social involvement of a political kind in something that might otherwise seem quite unconnected, it is necessary to consider an example. The most striking example, and perhaps the easiest to understand, of the use that new left thinkers have made of these insights, is the interpretation of mental breakdown as essentially a social, and ultimately a political, matter. This example is useful precisely because it seems, at first sight, to have nothing to do with politics.[1]

First of all, it has to be noticed that in the natural sciences the area of enquiry that is under review consists of 'inert' facts. That is to say, they are not altered by the presence of the observer as he does the investigation, and he is not altered by them. Or, at any rate— with the possible exception of micro-physics, in which the notorious 'uncertainty principle' reigns[2]—if there is any alteration, it is irrelevant to the purpose and success of the investigation. (A physicist may happen to be overcome with emotion at the beauty of some optical phenomenon, but this does not give him any new facts to be taken into account in his formulation of a theory to account for it.) But in an investigation of a human, personal problem, the presence of a personal relation between the subject and the investigator inevitably gives a colouring to the whole enquiry. The intrusion of one person into the life of another is what actually furnishes the data on which the whole enquiry proceeds. The disturbance that the intrusion causes is the sole source of the facts of the case insofar as they

[1] Most of this work has been done by the psychiatrists R. D. Laing and David Cooper. The most accessible exposition is the 1965 Pelican edition of R. D. Laing's *The Divided Self*, London 1959, but other works include: R. D. Laing and David Cooper, *Reason and Violence*, London 1964; R. D. Laing, *The Self and Others*, London 1961; and R. D. Laing and A. Esterson, *Sanity, Madness and the Family*, London 1964. See also two articles by David Cooper: 'Two Types of Rationality', *New Left Review* 29 (January–February 1965), 62–8; and 'Violence in Psychiatry', *Views* 8 (Summer 1965), 18–24.

[2] Even here, Cooper argues, the main point still stands: 'mathematical techniques . . . maintain the observer in some sort of exteriority to the observed' ('Two Types of Rationality', 62).

can be known to the investigator. For until he meets and talks to his subject he cannot even begin his work. The facts to be observed, then, are not *inert* in such an enquiry. They are themselves continually shifting under the varying pressures of the human relationship that alone reveals them.

It might be argued here that this is only true of an intimate, personal relationship, such as that between the psychiatrist and his patient. Surely, it will be said, this is not true of a purely statistical enquiry, such as might be undertaken by a sociologist who is concerned with general trends of behaviour on a large scale. This point depends for its force on treating people precisely as if they *were* inert, and as if their behaviour *were* predictable in the same way that the behaviour of stones or waves is predictable. Human behaviour, in the mass, is only relatively predictable (not absolutely) because, given a large enough sample, the variations that arise from the exercise of human freedom cancel each other out. But it is part of the presupposition of a fully human study, i.e, a study of free persons as such, that the subject can, if he wishes, alter his behaviour in accordance with his own awareness of the process that he is undergoing in the course of the study itself. He is, in this sense, not just a natural object, but a being who is intrinsically superior to nature, able to behave freely, and not necessarily subject to laws which override him.

It follows from this that a study of a human being cannot be just the study of a completed 'totality'. This point needs clarification. We can grasp a purely natural object as a completed whole. This is not to say that it may not, in the future, change. But here and now we can grasp it as it *is*, and so handle it conceptually. This chair or that tree are completed wholes, and this is why I can talk about them as, respectively *this* chair and *that* tree. Of course, the tree may grow, and change its shape; or the chair may break and be chopped up into firewood. But in both cases I can comprehend the general law of growth, or the possibility of disintegration, which govern objects of this kind, without any particular reference to this unique example. Trees grow, but only in the way that they *naturally* grow. But a man does not merely grow and change according to biological law. He changes himself, by his own conscious action. He never completely falls into any one conceptual framework. A person, being a unique conscious and self-determining centre, is unique in a special way. He forges his own uniqueness. He is never completed, and every concept of him is inadequate, and arrests him in his tracks. In reality he is always on the move, making and remaking himself. And this process of perpetual self-making is not subject to any naturally discoverable law. For as soon as a law about man, whether as an individual person or as a society, is formulated, the person who knows it is able to *choose* whether to 'obey' it or not. Thus, when somebody evolves a sociological 'law' that all men are bound by their class-position to live in a certain way, an individual can immediately decide to live in a different way and so defy the 'law'. Or again, a psychiatrist may find a law which says that all schizophrenics are incapable of looking after themselves—a schizophrenic has only to go and live on his own to disprove it.

This last example may be illuminating. Why is it

that we feel more inclined to suppose that the law about schizophrenics cannot be broken than that concerning normal people? Because we feel that schizophrenia is a breakdown of a mechanism—an illness a person has which robs him of some of his freedom. Schizophrenia, like (say) diabetes, limits a person's scope of choice and behaviour. But with diabetes there is a clear, stable relationship between the illness and the kind of behaviour it limits. Diabetes does not prevent me from choosing to read Shakespeare rather than Plato, but it does prevent me from going about without insulin for long. That is to say, there is an explicable, observed connection between the kind of condition and the kind of behaviour it affects. But with schizophrenia there is no stable connection. To try to distinguish a person's inability to play the piano from his inability to love his wife, by saying that the second is clearly due to his schizophrenic 'illness'' while the first is not, would be to go beyond the warrant of the observed evidence. Indeed, according to the existentialist psychiatrist, it is impossible to understand schizophrenia at all if we think of it as a specific kind of breakdown in a complex human mechanism, even if we try to clarify this by calling it a specifically *mental*, or psychological, mechanism that has collapsed. For the real question is not what *sort* of illness the schizophrenic has got (is it physical? is it mental? or is it psycho-somatic, i.e, a bit of both?). The question is whether schizophrenia is an illness *one* person has at all. Clearly schizophrenia is a breakdown *somewhere*. But is it in the individual subject, or in the relationship that shows up in contact with the doctor? Or is it perhaps only an outcrop of some far more pervasive social malaise—the kind of social sickness that Marx calls 'alienation'?[1]

The fact is that one can try to understand what is wrong here in two different and incompatible ways, according to two different conceptual frameworks.

[1] For a full understanding of this concept, a thorough reading of Marx is necessary: but the two following quotations indicate the main thought, as Marx formulated it, and show that according to Marx's interpretation alienation is not a subjective personal feeling but an objective social condition:

'The more the worker expends himself in work, the more powerful becomes the world of objects which he creates in face of himself, and the poorer he himself becomes in his inner life, the less he belongs to himself. It is just the same as in religion. The more of himself man attributes to God, the less he has left in himself. The worker puts his life into the object, and his life then belongs no longer to him but to the object. The greater his activity, therefore, the less he possesses. . . . The *alienation* of the worker in his product means not only that his labour becomes an object, takes on its own existence, but that it exists outside him, independently, and alien to him, and that it stands opposed to him as an autonomous power. The life which he has given to the object sets itself against him as an alien and hostile force.

'In what does . . . alienation of labour consist? First, that the work is external to the worker, that it is not a part of his nature, that consequently he does not fulfil himself in his work but denies himself, has a feeling of misery, not of wellbeing, does not develop freely a physical and mental energy, but is physically exhausted and mentally debased. The worker therefore feels himself at home only during his leisure, whereas at work he feels homeless. His work is not voluntary, but imposed, forced labour. It is not the satisfaction of a need, but only a means for satisfying other needs. Its alien character is clearly shown by the fact that as soon as there is no physical or other compulsion it is avoided like the plague. Finally, the alienated character of work for the worker appears in the fact that it is not his work but work for someone else, that in work he does not belong to himself but to another person.

'Just as in religion the spontaneous activity of human fantasy, of the human brain and heart, reacts independently, that is, as an alien activity of gods or devils, upon the individual, so the activity of the worker is not a spontaneous activity. It is another's activity, and a loss of his own spontaneity.'

(*Economic and Philosophical Manuscripts* 1844)

(Just as one can see the diagram on this page either as a black cross on a white ground, or as a white flower on a black ground, but not both at once.) A choice has to be made. Either one can think of the person as one who 'has an illness', in which case one will listen to him, in order to discover, in the jumble of 'nonsense' he appears to be uttering, some symptoms of the kind of illness he has. Or one can try to listen to what he says on the assumption that he is still a free person, capable of self-expression, who, though what he says may seem strange to 'us', is giving us a valid account of how he feels. That is to say, he has to be taken seriously, not just because otherwise we cannot cure him, but because he is still a human being freely choosing to say what he says because it seems to him to be *true*. If we assume, simply from the apparent incoherence or extravagance of his talk, that he must be 'mad' (that is to say, lacking that capacity for distinguishing truth which the 'sane' person enjoys) *we*—the 'sane' community—have already given our relationship to him an interpretation of our own. We have chosen to see him as, in a certain sense, no longer free to speak the truth about himself, but have pigeonholed him in a category which separates him from normal persons. Hence we are forced to understand his talk as merely *symptomatic* of his condition, rather than as a valid *description* of his condition.

The important point is that this interpretation, which we have chosen to give to the situation, is one that we are not, in any sense, forced to make. It does not spring self-evidently from a mere inspection of the facts. We choose to see him thus, because we too have some motive or cause for doing so—and perhaps what really needs examination is the nature and basis of this motive. Why do 'we' *want* to see 'him' as a being to be pigeonholed in this way, and so separated from us? What validity has this relationship of 'us' and 'him'? Perhaps it is the very distance that 'we' want to put between ourselves and the 'mad' person that prevents us from understanding and helping him.

Now, both patient and doctor belong to wider communities—those of 'the insane' and of 'the medical profession'. And these communities, each with its own distinctive structure of attitudes and presuppositions about the other, belong also to society in the general sense, with *its* structures and attitudes. To some degree all these attitudes and presuppositions influence and determine the relationship between the patient and the psychiatrist. Indeed, even to talk of the *patient* is to structure the relation in such a way as to think of one participant as passive and the other active, the one as simply receiving treatment and the other as giving it. And this may prevent the psychiatrist from helping his patient. Perhaps there is a need for the patient to be active and the psychiatrist to receive the impact of his action, not just as a therapeutic tactic by a doctor who remains all the while in total control, but as a genuine compassion which deliberately risks loss of that 'control'.

Thus it may legitimately be said that the whole of society is, to some degree, involved in the 'mad' person's predicament. We cannot set a limit to the 'situation' which is expressed in the consulting room. That is only the tip of an iceberg. If it is the pressure of wider society which has subtly forced a particular structural interpretation on an artificially limited situation, then perhaps it is the wider society which is really in need of treatment. Perhaps society, rather than the individual, is sick and in need of a cure. Perhaps the individual is only the weak point in a faulty social substructure—he is the point at which the lava of social disorder flows to the surface and is identified. His 'madness' is then ours. We tend to think of *him* as alone in need of cure partly because we want to disguise this truth from ourselves. To think of madness as a disease that one person has, and another does not have, is a kind of bad faith on the part of a society which does not want to face the ugly truth about itself: namely, that it is in need of some kind of total restructuring which might finally remove the faults in the present order.

Thus the argument turns inevitably to politics (in the comprehensive sense). To interpret schizophrenia as a free expression of a human condition that involves society as a whole, is to see it in political terms. And conversely, to see it as just an individual illness is to make a contrary political assumption. To label a person as 'mad' is to outlaw him because the cost of doing anything else, in terms of compassion, understanding, self-awareness, and commitment to total structural change, is too great to be faced. The way we think about madness is a sign of the way we think about the whole human order and its possibilities. It is part of a theory of man.

This argument about schizophrenia could be followed up in many different ways, in order to show the implications of the attempt to work out a humanism that would refuse to categorise, limit, and finally enslave man in the limits of a single set of concepts. It would have been possible to start a discussion of the kind of humanism the new left has been trying to work out from a quite other beginning than this. Problems such as crime, bad industrial relations, dissatisfactions in work or family life, the expression of human aggression in civil or international conflict, could all be misconstrued in purely naturalistic, scientific terms, or they could be considered in the properly humanistic framework. I have chosen madness because it seems at first to most people to have so little to do with politics. I shall now only briefly carry the train of thought further, in two directions that are relevant for a study of the catholic left.

The first concerns the limits of a purely scientific, objective study of human personality in general. For the biologist or physiologist, another person is a complex, living, but wholly exterior, object—a piece of biological machinery. I am an object of the physiologist's investigation; yet, as he studies me, as a bodily object, the physiologist does not at the same time investigate himself in the same way.[1] He is aware of himself, of course, in the sense that he is feeling and probing and questioning me with his own hands. But he is not attending to the structure of *his* own hands and eyes in the way that he is studying me. Indeed, he cannot think of himself in the same terms that he thinks of me. There have to be two different conceptual frameworks for a man to be able to think coherently about himself. The first is that of the self considered simply as an inert object laid out in front of an investigator, a part of nature. I can even consider myself in this way if I wish, and perhaps 'use' myself according to that mode of apprehension. But since I am a self-conscious being all the time that I am doing this, and since it is from myself—to use an awkward expression—that all my investigations flow, I need some other conceptual framework to comprehend myself as the source of this very study that I am undertaking. But to get such a conceptual framework

[1] He may, of course, as part of his own studies, subject his own body to investigation and analysis. But even when, say, he gives himself an injection, to see what effect it has on his liver, he is doing this as one who is, for the time being, concentrating on some particular piece of himself as if that part were part of someone else—an *object* in the same sense as other people's livers are objects for him.

clear is extremely difficult: I am for every escaping my own intellectual grasp.[1]

The importance of understanding this train of thought is that it leads towards a certain reverence for persons, especially for persons as they are related to me. Just as you have to be an object within my field of vision in order that I can see you as a genuinely other person, and so respect you for that uniqueness, so also I have to realise that I too am an object in your eyes. I have to accept the humiliation that, in a sense, this recognition forces on me. The whole basis of inter-personal relationships is thus founded upon our re-membering that we are, necessarily and simultane-ously, both objects and subjects. Both conceptual frameworks are necessary. To lose sight of either of them, or to try to describe people in terms of one of them only, is to enter upon a dangerous and slippery path. To imagine that people are describable entirely, and in principle, in purely scientific humanist terms is to be in danger of treating them as objects. They be-come mere counters in the sight of some purely non-natural, superior viewer who is not, himself, an object for investigation or criticism. It is to treat human beings, and human values, as *things*. (This is what, in Marx's jargon, is called *reification*. His insight in this matter is as significant as it was in the case of under-standing human relationships previously in terms of

[1] It is necessary to emphasise once again here that these two 'conceptual frameworks' do not correspond to two differ-ent *parts* of a compound personality—i.e., to body and spirit —but rather to two different points of view from which the one, undivided person can be understood. The duality lies in the different frames of reference used, not in the subject using them.

alienation.) On the other hand, to suppose that we are essentially just subjective consciousnesses and not intrinsically solid spatial objects, is also to devalue human beings. The fact that this kind of thinking has often been applauded, on the grounds that it offers a superior, more 'spiritual' idea of man, only goes to show how easily the plain falsity of a philosophical attitude can be mistaken for a kind of profundity. A 'spiritualisation' of man which tries to ignore his bodily condition is simply a lie, and cannot in any way be regarded as superior to a view which sees man as he is, with all his earthiness.

More important than this, even, is the fact that it is his bodiliness which is the source both of man's community and of his tragic isolation. Human community is a society of bodies which are present to each other. It is in our bodiliness that we share the same life, partake of the same food and live in the same place. In this sharing we see that a man cannot be alone by himself, since he in fact shares his very bodiliness with other people. Bodiliness ties us all up together in the bundle of life, as the Jews well understood—and as the modern biblical scholar insists too, in christian terms.[1] But there is also a sense in which the body is what divides us from each other. Of course death is the epitome of this isolation of the person in his body. But isolation is a fact of human existence throughout life too. The aspiration of lovers to transcend their mutual separation in a bodily unity is, at best, only transitorily achieved. The potentially tragic dimensions of this fact are clear. In human love, understood not only in the

[1] See, for example, J. A. T. Robinson, *The Body*, London 1952, 29.

sexual sense but also in the political sense (i.e, as the desire for the creation of a political community of free persons united in one body), man's urge towards over-coming the paradoxical duality of his condition be-comes apparent. He can only comprehend himself under separate and even incompatible aspects, dis-tinct conceptual frameworks each appropriate only to some portion of his total experience. To try to elimin-ate the tension that exists between these, or to interpret everything in terms of one framework alone, is to invite failure and to degrade humanity to something less complex than it really is. Yet man cannot help attempting to unify his experience. It is part of his freedom that he should try to transcend the limits of his situation. To understand this and see its potential tragedy is to grasp the essential truth of the kind of humanism that the new left is trying to formulate.

The second aspect of the humanistic philosophy that I want to consider is its concept of language. Just as we have two concepts of the person, so we need two concepts of language. The difference between these two concepts can best be illustrated with one or two examples. The first example is taken from the philo-sophical part of Raymond Williams's *The Long Revo-lution*, in which he is discussing a creative—as op-posed to a merely imitative—theory of the nature of art, and of the process of artistic production. He first of all points out that:

We learn to see a thing by learning to describe it; this is the normal process of perception, which can only be seen as complete when we have interpreted the incoming sen-sory information either by a known configuration or rule, or by some new configuration which we can try to learn as a new rule.[1]

Now the familiar rules, and the new rules that we may be able to learn, in order to describe what we see, are both socially given. For it is the language that we are born into that is the repository of these socially created rules. Only in accordance with them are we able to describe and so to see the world around us.

We must start from the position that reality *as we experience it* is in this sense a human creation; that all our experience is a human version of the world we inhabit.[2]

Yet clearly this cannot be altogether true, and Williams's own words themselves show us why. For there *is* a sense in which we do see first and describe afterwards, just as there is a sense in which we describe first and see afterwards. Or rather, it is not a question of temporal priorities, but of a simultaneous interconnection.

This interplay of opposed emphases works both ways. If Williams is right to emphasise the flow from verbal description to thing seen, my second example (from Orwell) emphasises the flow in the other direction:

When you think of a concrete object, you think wordlessly, and then, if you want to describe the thing you have been visualising you probably hunt about till you find the exact words that seem to fit it. When you think of something abstract you are more inclined to use words

[1] Raymond Williams, *The Long Revolution*, London 1961 (p. 39 of the 1965 Pelican edition).
[2] Williams, *The Long Revolution*, 35.

from the start, and unless you make a conscious effort to prevent it, the existing dialect will come rushing in and do the job for you, at the expense of blurring or even changing your meaning.[1]

If you want to be free, then, you must not become the slave of the language that is given to you.

Now it is clear that the opposed emphases of these two passages reflect more than opposed linguistic theories, or even opposed habits of composition: they reflect opposed *political* trends or attitudes. What Williams is concerned to argue for is the fact that, in our use of language, we express our intrinsic solidarity with each other, our inability even to see the world except within a social context which provides us with the tools for seeing. Orwell, however, is concerned to defend the human individual's chance of standing free from what he sees as a threatening social milieu, and of seeing *for himself*, autonomously, what the world is like. Clearly, an adequate philosophy of language must take into account both of these complementary, and equally necessary, truths. But even to put it like that is inadequate. For it is not that they are equal and opposite truths, to be held in a kind of extrinsic balance with each other. We do not want to be continually rushing from one to the other in a perpetual effort to retain a sane view of things. Rather we want to say that they are simultaneously valid. But is it possible to state this deeper single truth, that is supposed to contain both emphases, except by simply reiterating them both and at the same time denying their mutual contradiction? And if it is possible, how

[1] George Orwell, 'Politics and the English Language', *Collected Essays*, London 1961, 359.

do we state it? If not, what kind of truth is this, that cannot be stated?

A closer examination of both arguments will help here. In both cases there is, in fact, a kind of inbuilt contradiction even within the single view. Thus Williams maintains that 'reality *as we experience it* is in this sense a human creation'. It is easy to see the point he is trying to make. He does not want to be accused of supposing, like Bishop Berkeley, that we have no reason to suppose anything exists except when we are looking at it. Reality is not subjective in that sense. Hence he underlines 'as we experience it' to make this point. There is, he implies, a reality in itself, not seen by us, and this is not a human creation. But to say this immediately contradicts a central point of his argument, which is that in fact reality as we do *not* experience it is unstateable, and we cannot talk about it at all—not even to say that it does or does not exist. A similar puzzle arises when he goes on to say that 'all our experience is a human version of the world we inhabit'. This, once more, suggests that there is some sense in which there is a world altogether independent of our experience. Our experience is just a *version* of this world. But what is this world that is independent of us? And how is our experience a version of it? How are we to know whether our version is a true or false one? There is clearly a difficulty here. We see that Williams is getting at an important idea. But in order to say it, he has to use concepts that, in the very saying of it, suggest the opposite.

Exactly the same kind of objection can be raised about Orwell's view. He speaks of finding words that 'exactly fit' the wordless thought that you first have of the object. But what sense can be made of this notion of a word *fitting* a thought? How can you tell whether it is a bad fit or a good one, except by comparing it with another 'fit' which is somehow better or worse? But then the same puzzle arises about *that* 'fit' that we found in the first case, and so we are no better off. In fact, the notion of a word 'fitting' a thought—borrowed as it clearly is from some such notion as that of a hat fitting or not fitting a particular head—is strictly unintelligible. Words and thoughts are not objects that can be compared with each other for a good or bad fit: they are not objects at all. To learn a word's meaning, and use it, is indeed to learn a thought: but that simply means that we learn the thought by using the word, in the given language. All the same, what Orwell says *does* make sense of a kind. We can to some extent distinguish accurate from inaccurate descriptions. Orwell's essay is a lesson in how to do this in the case of political descriptions. The fact is that it is hard, if not downright impossible, not to find oneself having to use some terminology which suggests words 'fitting' thoughts in some spatial or other 'objective' sense, even when one is trying to say something that itself cannot be 'fitted' to the thought in that way.[1]

[1] It may be worth mentioning, for the benefit of any readers who have philosophical inclinations, that it is perhaps possible to interpret the philosophy of Wittgenstein as an attempt to reconcile these two views of language. The *Tractatus* is the most subtle and ingenious example ever devised of a theory of language as 'words fitting thoughts', but it founders on just the kind of difficulty I have discussed. In the *Philosophical Investigations*, the other—social—concept of language is elaborated, but as a result the whole of the *Tractatus*, including some points which seem to be valid, have to go by the board. Wittgenstein's work has the quality of tragedy, and the eloquence of tragedy, for this reason.

In these two examples we can see clearly not only the philosophical problem of language—its seeming insolubility and paradoxicality—but also the political importance. For the two examples come directly out of a difference of political stance. And in their clash they reflect, I think, the difficulties of the socialist humanism the new left is trying to formulate. Each emphasis attempts, in the name of a genuine political and moral awareness, to overcome the paradox of human language which simultaneously binds together and keeps apart human beings. Each tries actually to eliminate the truth that is inherent in the other. The danger of Williams's view is that, in its concern for man's social milieu, it may actually deny the existence (and perhaps eventually the right to existence) of the individual person. The reality of the danger is evidenced by Perry Anderson, who goes further, and less warily than Williams, when he says:

'Society' and the 'individual' are both essentialist abstractions, based on the notion that persons and institutions are closed, demarcated *beings*, with fixed boundaries between them. In reality, there are no such separate, autarchic beings—there is instead a continuum of human *actions*, which collide, converge, and coalesce to form the whole personal and social world we live in.[1]

In other words, words such as *person*, or *individual*, or *society* are not substantives, referring to entities, but adjectives, qualifying a kind of life. Life itself then becomes the only subject of either social or personal existence. Now one can understand the importance of this as an *emphasis*; especially the emphasis that, *if*

[1] Anderson, 'Problems of Socialist Strategy', 288.

'society' is an abstraction, then, *for the same kind of reason*, 'the individual' is an abstraction too. Raymond Williams makes a similar point, but with greater sensitivity, in *The Long Revolution*. There he traces the history of the process by which, in our own day, the terms *individual* and *society* have come to refer to independent entities. But, significantly, his actual conclusion is the opposite of Anderson's. Whereas for Anderson, both *individual* and *society* are abstractions from a single reality to which they refer, for Williams the abstract character of these two terms is the result of our own cultural and political failure to relate them. By trying to understand the individual as if he were a bare, autonomous, self-subsistent creature without intrinsic relationship to other people—i.e, to 'society'— we have turned what is in fact a genuine reality, a valid and concrete individual subject, into a mere abstraction. And in doing this to the 'individual', we have done the same to 'society' too. Instead of being, in reality, simply other people in their structural relationships, 'society' has become a kind of hypostatised object in its own right, and is divorced from any sense of the concrete rights and duties of real people.

In the contrast between these two views of Williams and Anderson as to how we should describe society, and the individuals who make it up, we can see, epitomised, the potential split between two interpretations of socialist humanism. For Williams does, in fact, maintain a sense of the reality and paradoxicality of the *society–individual* polarity, despite the unconsciously contradictory language he uses. Whereas Anderson seems to be trying to eliminate this paradox by proposing something that really *is* a pure abstraction:

namely, what he calls 'a collection of human *actions*, which collide, converge, and coalesce to form the whole personal and social world we live in'. It is perfectly obvious that in this phrase the notion of actions which, according to the previous sentence already quoted, are the actions not of 'separate autarchic beings' but of 'essentialist abstractions' is as problematic and paradoxical as the other notions already discussed. Indeed, the paradox that Anderson claims to be solving is actually *exemplified* in the terms he proposes to solve it with. This fact is, I think, connected with a point made earlier,[1] namely that, in trying to concentrate on theoretical questions of political philosophy and humanist ideology, the sense of concrete practical application has tended to be overshadowed in recent new left writing. The dangers of this process are now apparent. In the very name of a new kind of socialist humanism, the new left may be in danger of writing off, as abstractions, the real people for whom the work is being done.

All this philosophical analysis may seem unnecessarily abstract and divorced from the main political interest of the new left. But it would be a mistake to draw that conclusion. For the opposed emphases that we have noticed about the relationship of language to thought, word to thing, reflect very clearly the differences between 'individualism' and the kind of humanism the new left is trying to substitute for it. And that distinction is implicitly political because of the problems it raises about the kind of political analysis that is possible, within the two sets of terms. Thus an individualist like Orwell sees politics as a matter of

[1] See pp. 22–6 above.

manipulating institutions and organisations. He wants to be able to maintain that, necessary though political activity is, there is still a great deal of human life—perhaps the most important parts of it in fact—that lies beyond politics. For Williams, such an emphasis —based as it is on the narrow definition of politics—is not only conceptually inadequate, but politically defeatist and reactionary, however understandable and eloquent Orwell's own defence of it was. It is conceptually inadequate because it fails to give due attention to the total interpenetration between the individual's personal possibilities and the framework of institutional structures that sustains them. It is defeatist because, instead of seeing the need to transform these structures radically if the quality of personal individual life is to be adequately valued, it turns away from that task in order to try to build up a private existence which, in fact, cannot be sustained on that basis at all.

2. *A revolutionary humanism*

Socialist humanism as I have described it holds to the idea of a *revolutionary* politics. A political vision based on liberal reform, or any law of piecemeal evolution towards socialism, is felt to be inadequate. But I hope the previous pages have shown that an attempt has been made by some new left writers to get rid of the impression of vestigial bolshevism that J. M. Cameron detected in the original new left. The significance of Raymond Williams's title *The Long Revolution* is that, in the book, he tries to show that, though it may be long, and though it may not be violent in the sense in which, say, the revolutions in the developing countries are still violent, it is still a revolution, not just a reform, that western capitalist societies need. It is not always easy to see what the distinction actually amounts to. But in essence, it consists of the assertion that nothing short of a total change, undertaken through a single comprehensive strategy, will do. The difference between reform and revolution is not in the violence of the action, or the length, or the pace of change. It is that reform is piecemeal, taking one step at a time, and eschews an overall strategy altogether, while revolution is a total strategy for change.[1]

In order to discuss the new left conception of revolution I shall take, as a basic statement of the case, Raymond Williams's recent book *Modern Tragedy*. This work is an attempt to show: first, how what we are prepared to call tragic at any particular epoch is largely conditioned by our general outlook and system of values; and secondly, that today, in thinking of all social revolution as necessarily and intolerably tragic (as we in fact tend to think of it, and for this reason shy away from it), we are ourselves the victims of an anti-revolutionary ideology that is hindering us in our most important task: namely, to undertake the revolutionary action that is needed in order that man may be able to advance forward to a condition of true and total freedom in accordance with his own potentialities. Thus a reinterpretation of the traditional ways of

[1] It would be an injustice to give the impression, however, that the new left thinks the 'long revolutions' needed in advanced societies can be analysed or carried through without constant reference to the revolutionary movements that are going on in other parts of the world.

thinking about tragedy, both as an art-form and as an ordinary fact of life, is necessary if we are to overcome the main cultural and mental obstacle to the achievement of socialism. I shall not dwell at length on the literary criticism that this work involves, since it has already been subjected to close critical scrutiny, in a way that is extremely relevant to the theme of this book, by Walter Stein.[1] What I shall concentrate on is Williams's theoretical basis: i.e, his attempt to resolve the tragedy of a revolutionary political action which, as I have already hinted, seems to lie deep in the paradoxical character of the relationship of individual and society.

It is a presupposition of Williams's work that the liberation which a successful revolutionary action would bring would be total and at the same time altogether secular. It would be man's redemption of himself by himself. The redemptive process that this 'long revolution' would be, would not entail any discontinuities, such as the entrance into the human situation of a god or redeemer from beyond the human world. If one takes it for granted that all social disorder is ultimately remediable, any view that seems to contradict this—for instance, one in which the tragedy is blamed, not on man's own disorganisation and failure, but on 'fate'—has to be interpreted away, in terms of the social pressures that led to tragedy being viewed in that light. At certain crucial points the difficulties of this secular humanist thesis emerge, as Walter Stein

---

[1] In a series of three articles, published in *New Blackfriars* XLVIII, 561 and 562 (February and March 1967): 'Humanism and Tragic Redemption', 230–44; 'Redemption and Revolution', 319–26; and in *Slant* 15 (June–July 1967): 'Redemption and Tragic Transcendence', 3–10.

convincingly shows. This is especially true of the treatment of death, which Williams tries to convince us is not the tragic, lonely negation that it has been taken to be by most of the European tradition. 'To say that man dies alone is not to state a fact but to offer an interpretation,' Williams suggests:

However men die, the experience is not only the dissolution and ending; it is also a change in the lives and relationships of others, for we know death as much in the experience of others as in our own expectations and endings. And just as death enters, continually, in our common life, so any death is in a common language and depends on common experience.[1]

This view of death repeats the same emphasis that we have seen already in discussing Williams's concept of language. We have to describe death in order to see it, and the description we give will be taken from a common linguistic stock, or at any rate it will be made out of elements that are available in that stock.

True enough: but we can see, despite the validity of the point that is being made, another point that is not intended, but is in fact being made too. To say that a man dies alone is, certainly, an interpretation: but to say that it is *not* a fact is, in one important and obvious sense, just false. Or, at least, it is false if we assume that the whole notion of a fact which is not already an interpretation, but is somehow prior to all interpretations that have been put upon it, is a nonsensical notion. Such an assumption, moreover, seem to be required by Williams's general theory that '*all* our experience is a human version of the world we inhabit'.

[1] Raymond Williams, *Modern Tragedy*, London 1966, 57.

Death, then, is an interpretation or 'human version' because all experience is interpretation. There are no uninterpreted facts. But in that case, to say that death is not a fact but an interpretation is to put the point misleadingly, since it suggests a difference between two possible ways of putting it when one of them is impossible.

Yet, once more, it is hard to see how the point could be put in any other way that would not be open to the same kind of objection. What I am insisting on here is not that what Williams says is wrong, but that it will not bear being subsumed into a general description that is made in terms of only one overall conceptual framework. The notions of *fact* and *interpretation*, like the notions of *individual* and *society*, belong to different conceptual frameworks, and these cannot be put together without strain and loss of essential overtones and stresses. The attempt to do so has to be made: but at the same time we have to recognise and allow for the fact that it cannot be completely successful.

A very important element in Williams's whole theory of tragedy is that there is nothing absolutely and unavoidably tragic in the human condition. His basic view is that of Brecht: 'The sufferings of this man appal me, because they are unnecessary.' The idea of tragedy leads to the idea of revolution for just that reason:

In most modern drama, the best conclusion is: yes, this is how it was. Only an occasional play goes further, with the specific excitement of recognition: yes, this is how it is. Brecht, at his best, reaches out to, and touches the necessary next stage: yes, this is how it is, for these reasons, but the action is continually being replayed, and it could be otherwise.[1]

Thus the ordinary attitude of tragedy is to recognise, in the particular action, a general condition that is fundamental and unavoidable. Or rather, it is at any rate unavoidable given the circumstances of the case—and these circumstances, or others like them, are bound to recur at some time or another. Hence the universal significance of tragedy. But for Brecht, the marxist, and for Williams, the man of the new left, this is not necessarily true. The circumstances do not necessarily have to recur, for how we interpret them is our choice, part of our own freedom. We do not have to subscribe to a pessimistic view of tragedy. Tragedy, regarded as inevitable, is not simply a passive response to an inert fact, but an active grasping of a set of meanings that are already given, and limited, by the circumstances themselves. If we interpret the facts in one way, we shall see tragedy as inevitable. It is our choice. If we interpret them in another way, we shall see them as avoidable. And to see them in this latter way must lead, on the part of any sensitive person, to doing everything in his power to ensure that they don't occur again.

It is in the light of some such train of thought as this that Williams accepts the notion of revolution. For it is a necessary part of socialist humanism to hold that the circumstances of tragedy are not merely avoidable, but are our doing and our responsibility. The circumstances are the expression of the kind of society we have made and are helping to preserve. They are not

[1] Williams, *Modern Tragedy*, 202.

separable, in their apparent particularity, from the whole body of the social experience in which they are set. (Just as the situation of the schizophrenic is not only his situation, but part of a situation that confronts everybody in the society.) This is why it is our duty to do more than just deal with these tragic situations piecemeal. We have to attack the tragic element in human life on all the fronts simultaneously, for only in this way will the circumstances be actually changed, and be seen to be indefinitely changeable in the future, because only in a socialist humanist world will man be free to change his circumstances as he wishes. And to try to mount this attack is to commit oneself precisely to the revolutionary idea.

I have already briefly indicated what seems to me to be a central flaw that the socialist humanist of the new left has failed to notice in its programme for a total secular redemption of humanity. This is the irreducibility of the tension, or distance, between the two conceptual frameworks that are required for the erection of socialist humanism itself. This tension runs along the whole front, dividing as it does the naturalistic from the humanistic, the object world from the human world. The energy and persistence of new left thinking has been largely due to a desire—endemic, I think, in being human at all—to overcome this fundamental tension, and to find a single framework that will do for all aspects of human experience.

It is important to insist, from a christian point of view, on the extreme importance and relevance of this effort. For it is intolerable to be faced with the absurdity of having to admit defeat at this point. The whole aspiration of man, in his intellectual, his sexual, his emotional life, is for a mode of experience that will give him back his own unity, and that of the world in which he finds himself. But, as I have tried to show, in the nature of the case the attempt cannot completely succeed. It is simply impossible to state this unity except in terms that are irreducibly dualistic. One way out of this dilemma—which is, of course, not a solution, but an admission of defeat—is to give up trying, to make something of this defeat by asserting that it is either meaningless or idiotic to try. But perhaps there is another perspective, in which man is not confined to the limits of his own conceptual frameworks for ever, or throughout all the dimensions of his life. If man cannot overcome, by his own initiative, the dualism of the very terms in which his most fundamental drive to unity has to be expressed, perhaps this means that man cannot and should not be content to rest on his own resources. May it be that what is lacking in socialist humanism to make it consistent and acceptable is just that belief in a redemption from beyond man's world which at present cannot be acknowledged? The whole meaning of the rise of the catholic left is that it is an attempt to show how that suggestion can be given a valid meaning in contemporary terms.

It is at this point that the most critical problem arises. For it is fundamental to the whole socialist-humanist view of life that man's redemption, however it be achieved, is a total redemption. This follows from the attempt that is made to interpret human existence within a set of ideas that are wholly self-consistent and which offer a potentially homogeneous description of man and his world. The difference between revolution and reform is thus not just one of political strategy, of how to attain an agreed goal. The piecemeal character of political reformism is a reflection of the fundamental scepticism of the reformer as to the potentialities of his own efforts. He does not believe with any confidence in total redemption—certainly not within history, at any rate. (The christian reformer does indeed hold to an idea of total redemption, but places both the means and the reality of this redemption beyond history altogether.) The reformer is prepared to do everything that he believes human political energies can achieve: but that will not bring in the millennium, for he does not believe in any such thing.

On the other hand, the revolutionary thinker recognises that no issues can be properly tackled except within a framework of total redemption, within which alone any specific political act has its full meaning. The possibility of total redemption is therefore basic to his whole outlook, and is responsible for his revolutionary strategy. We have to recognise, I think, that this attempt at coherence and consistency is a genuine and true response to an aspiration which is ineradicable in man—the aspiration to understand, explain, and unify his experience. Without this aspiration, human life would scarcely exist; it is this that raises man above the animal level of piecemeal, unrelated experiences. To deny the validity of the revolutionary perspective altogether would, then, be to deny humanity itself, even if it were done in order to save man from his own pride and self-destructiveness. But it must also be admitted, I think, that the revolutionary thinker has several extremely difficult problems to face.

The most basic of these problems is the philosophical difficulty that I have already discussed: the impossibility of completely describing human experience in a single set of internally consistent concepts. But this difficulty generates others of a more immediate and practical kind. If he is a christian, or a believer in the possibility of total redemption only through some external, superhuman power, the revolutionary has to show why it is that man cannot just resign himself to the coming of that power. That is to say, if political action cannot, ultimately, bring about the total redemption that he hopes for, then there is a problem of giving adequate importance to the relatively, but not absolutely, significant political actions that he does advocate. He has got to answer the charge that, by bringing in a power from outside politics, he is condemning the political action itself and taking away its raison d'être. This is not necessarily difficult. He can simply say that, humanly speaking, some political actions are demanded just on grounds of sheer justice and humanity.

But how is he to distinguish those strategies which lead towards the final redemptive act of God from others which do not? If there is a discontinuity between man's 'revolution' and God's 'resolution', how is man to see the way which leads from the one to the other? Is there anything available as a guide, other than the vaguest moral and human considerations? And if not—that is to say, if there is no absolutely valid law of history at work which can strictly dictate the details of political action—how are the various political choices that are made to be given the totality and coherence they need, if they are to constitute a genuine revolution? How is revolution to be distinguished from reform if there is a real choice of revolutionary ways forward, even from a particular concrete historical situation? Such a distinction can hardly be made without *forcing* an inference from some quite general moral, humane considerations to a particular political strategy—a forcing which the mechanism will not bear. (Sometimes, of course, general moral considerations do almost dictate a certain policy. One might say that sheer humanity dictated that Hitler be fought in Europe, or that the USA be opposed in Vietnam, or that special help be given to the poor families in Britain. But such inferences are valid only because the issue is regarded as, to a large extent, independent of other issues, and is in this sense not seen as part within a revolutionary perspective. In other words, the argument from a general morality to political revolution is weakest just where it needs to be strongest, and vice versa.)

If it is hard to see the precise connection between God's redemptive act and man's revolutionary activity, it is equally difficult to find out from history alone what are the right lines into the future. This is the special problem that the agnostic revolutionary has to face, though the christian, even if his perspective offers him the chance of an ultimate *intellectual* consistency, cannot evade having to face it too. Clearly there must be some limits to the total revolutionary action he demands, for without these the revolution cannot be grasped as a totality at all. Thus some criteria are necessary for distinguishing actions that are proper to the revolution from those that are not. Where are they to come from, if they are not to be just subjective, and hence open to instant and perpetual revision as occasion demands?

I do not offer a solution to either of these problems that face the revolutionary, since I do not think there is any. All that seems to be possible is for us to try to maintain a sense of the interconnectedness of the various political problems while at the same time choosing the priorities that we think most urgent and attending to them as they arise. In other words, we have to keep in mind the dangers attendant on both reformism and revolution, while recognising that neither is a consistent or adequate position if taken purely by itself. Reformism, *as a doctrine,* is inadequate because it does not answer to man's fundamental need for unity, coherence, and rationality. Indeed, the very act of erecting it into a doctrine witnesses to the inadequacy that reformism suffers from. Such an attempt itself exemplifies the aspiration that reformism itself refuses to acknowledge. It is possible to act in a reformist way, but it is impossible to *believe in reformism as a system.* For, by definition, there is in reformism nothing 'whole' to believe; and, in any case, few people are capable of that degree or kind of political opportunism. Nevertheless, the tendency to erect opportunism—by which I do not mean anything intrinsically bad, but merely the neutral notion of taking every issue as it comes and doing one's best with it—into a political philosophy is practically universal. And rightly so: for issues do not, in fact, just 'come', atomistically; we find them only as parts of a comprehensible historical pattern that we cannot help making for ourselves.

Revolution, on the other hand, is inadequate because—as I have argued—it demands things that it cannot have: namely, objective criteria and total self-consistency. However, the problem of revolutionary politics in a country like Britain is more concrete than this. It lies in the meaning that is to be given to such concepts as a 'long revolution', a 'non-violent revolution', and the like. These are concepts of great importance to a socialist humanism, for two reasons. One is that, for practical purposes, the notion of a short, violent, and bloody revolution in Britain is clearly irrelevant—and for that reason becomes, in practice, an evasion of the political problem. Hence, the only kind of revolution that can be supposed is one that is long, and probably not very violent by historical standards. The second reason is that, in the kind of world that we inhabit, the notion of any revolution that is both short and humane is hard to entertain. That such revolutions may still be inevitable, and indeed necessary, does not make them any the less tragic and in many ways contrary to the very standards of human value that a socialist humanism demands. Thus, while perhaps it is necessary to tolerate, and even support, violent revolutions in some places, any humanism worthy of the name needs to be able to give some sense to the notion of revolution that does not flagrantly deny the humanity that the revolution itself claims to redeem. The notion of a long, non-violent revolution must, for this reason, be shown to be somehow valid as a standard against which the real value of actual revolutions may be assessed, and in the name of which the actual costs, in terms of suffering and tragedy, can rightly and justifiably be paid.

But here again there is, it seems to me, a very real

difficulty. The notion of a long revolution—as used, for instance, in Raymond Williams's book of that name—is drawn from a survey of the past. That is to say, what was no doubt felt at the time to be a confused mass of unrelated actions, stretching over an indefinite period of history, can now be understood, in the light of our subsequent history, to constitute a coherent pattern. This coherence we may now, with hindsight, properly regard as revolutionary. But it is only at this distance that so large and ill-connected a mass of political activities, taking place in so many different spheres and under such different auspices, and for such different immediate ends, can be comprehended in a single view. If the idea of a long revolution depends in this sense upon its being mostly, if not all, in the past how can such a concept be of any use to us now, in trying to formulate a political strategy for the present and the future? Isn't it the case that only as long as an envisaged revolution is thought of as short, can it be comprehended as a totality—as it must be if it is to be truly revolutionary? To speak of a long revolution for the future is, perhaps, to speak of something that we cannot properly grasp. Certainly, the longer it is to be, the less revolutionary the idea of it becomes. For there is a real connection between the ideas of revolution and of speedy transformation, since only in a relatively short historical time-span can the totality of a complex mass of political actions be grasped, either mentally (as an idea) or in practice (as a task to be done).

The concept of a long revolution must therefore always be an interpretation of the past rather than an invitation to the future. Perhaps this means that the term can only be of use as rhetoric rather than as an exact concept. This does not mean that it has no validity. There *is* a difference between piecemeal political opportunism and the totality of political revolution. But it is perhaps a matter of degree rather than of kind. The more we are able to see the interconnectedness of projected actions in different fields, and seek to undertake them all simultaneously on a wide front, interpreting each in the light of the effect it has on others, the more revolutionary will our political stategy be. But there is no sharp theoretical line to be drawn between what is strictly proper to revolution and what is not. There will always be room for real differences and doubts, and this fact must always be allowed for if the humanism in the name of which revolution is undertaken is not to be betrayed in the undertaking itself. To say that *this*, rather than *that*, policy is right just because it is the revolutionary one does not, by itself, settle anything of substance, even if it is granted that, in general, revolutionary policies are what the situation demands. This is the limitation to which any revolutionary politics is necessarily committed, and which any revolutionary political strategy will ignore at its peril.

3
The christian basis of the catholic left

When one considers all the fuss there has recently been about the catholic left, against the theological insights it has actually produced, their paucity becomes very obvious. Once the pleas for a renewed theology of this or that aspect of christianity have been acknowledged, what is left is not much more than a few, very general, propositions. This may seem a sufficiently damaging criticism to make, especially if one is trying to recommend the catholic left to a probably sceptical reader. But more has to be said even than this. For the catholic left has done little as yet, either, to convince non-christians of the left that *their* view of the faith—based often no doubt upon a popular, out-of-date, and soon discarded piety drawn from one denomination or another—is in any way in need of substantial modification.

To say this is harsh: but it needs to be said in order that the genuine significance of the catholic left be understood, and the scale of its future work measured. The claim I am making is that this is not just a small, half-spent movement whose life is already well advanced, and which will soon go the way of many other 'movements' in the church. The catholic left is not an already-mature but insignificant minority within the larger body of the church. It *is*, I would argue, the actual embryo of the church that is to come. As far as I can see, there is no other way than through the catholic left—understood not merely in its British context, but in the context of a widely scattered but mutually sympathetic set of groups throughout the world church—for christianity to survive. This is the real scale of the claim that has to be made, and supported by achievements in the future. It is against this responsibility that I have judged its present achievements. Against the standards of other ecclesiastical movements, of course, the achievement looks a good deal larger. But such standards are, in any case, no longer of much importance, since they belong essentially to the era that is passing and breaking up. (I am not here referring to standards of scholarly integrity or honesty, but standards of importance and relevance and value to the world as a whole.)

The theological—as distinct, I should say, from the philosophical and cultural—stance of the catholic left consists, when analysed, in a few key notions. The first is an eschatological idea: namely the identification—more or less complete—of the coming kingdom of the glorious and risen Lord with the establishment of a socialist society. The exact meaning of this identification is, obviously, of critical importance. But its general acceptance by the catholic left is a characteristic stance. The second idea is ecclesiological: it may be called (for the sake of any better term, and despite the proprietorial tones it may suggest here) the 'culture and liturgy' argument. This is an argument—of some complexity already, but surely ripe for refinement and amplification in due course—to the effect that, in the first place, the liturgy of the visible church here and now is a model by which we can determine the outline of what a humane political society ought to be; and, in the second place, that a close study of this model in the light of the actual context in which it is set—that is, in relation to the culture of its place and time—will show that it here and now involves a political commitment to socialism, as the visible expression, to the world, of the inner meaning of what it is to be a member of that liturgical community.

Linked to these ideas is a third: namely, that christianity involves a certain unfashionable moral intransigence in the face of what may seem revolutionary demands. This intransigence must not be understood in the old harsh terms of proposing and exacting an alien rule of behaviour, tied to severe external sanctions, and imposed upon a subject population. It is to be seen as the firm basis of a revolutionary impetus for radical social change. Moral intransigence is the christian contribution to the brechtian conception of the tragic. If 'that man's sufferings appal me because they are unnecessary', then, insofar as that is the case, the circumstances that made them necessary *must*, as a matter of absolute moral duty, be changed. (A morality which tries to tailor behaviour to the situation that actually presents itself to us has no intrinsic incentive to ensuring such change. It is liable to accept man's tragedy as absolute and final: and hence to be prepared to put up with it, bending whatever rules have to be bent in order to make the situation tolerable.) It is a basic insight of the catholic left that an intolerable situation—such as that by which peace is maintained by the threat of murder and genocide—is *not* to be tolerated, under any circumstances, and can in fact be changed given the political will and the right degree of persistence, intelligence and persuasiveness. Each of these key ideas needs to be examined in turn, and linked if possible to the political ideas already discussed.

1. Socialism and the kingdom of God

The clearest and most eloquent expression of this identification of socialism and the kingdom is that of Martin Redfern in the *Slant Manifesto*.[1] He tries to show that there is not only a parallel but an actual coalescence of ideas between the contemporary theology of the church and Marx's concept of *alienation* (see above, p. 39). For this reason, Marx's demand for the elimination of this pervasive social malaise, by the emancipation of the alienated class through revolution, is identified with the church's role in the world: namely, that of liberating men from their slavery to sin—sin now also understood as a pervasive social malaise. (What the New Testament writers might call bondage to the principalities and powers of this world, we can today more intelligibly refer to as alienation.)

Redfern works the idea out in some detail, and with a good deal of theological insight. He shows that the church has to be a closed society, limited in some way to a circle of persons who can genuinely be brotherly,

[1] Martin Redfern, 'The church, sacrament of a socialist society', *Catholics and the Left*, London 1966, 148–82.

and serve as an example and sign of the brotherliness that is required of all humanity. In this sense, the church is a society called out of the world, to be itself, and with its own intrinsic structure. But it has also, at the same time, to be open, in order that the brotherliness that is within it can be diffused, not by a process of imitation, but by a real *incorporation* into the one brotherhood of mankind. Thus 'the church is only there to serve the world; and, insofar as it does serve the world, it becomes one with the world, and to that extent ceases to be "church"'.[1] In this way, christianity is truly a rejection of 'religion', in the sense of a devotion just to some part of human experience only, however sublime and important that part may be. It is, in fact, a total commitment to the world.

So far, it might be said, Redfern has only expanded some remarks of J. M. Cameron on the new left in an article already cited:

The power of the Marxist myth lies in its being a myth of sin, suffering and redemption. The Fall in Marxism is the transition from primitive communism to class society. . . . The redemption, in the fullness of time, is the work of the most suffering class of modern society, the proletariat; and through the passion of the proletariat mankind passes into communism, a return to man's primitive integrity but at a higher level. Death is swallowed up in victory or, if with the Marxists, you prefer the categories of the Hegelian logic, the negation is negated.[2]

Shorn of the detachment and irony of this way of putting it, which scarcely does justice, perhaps, to the

[1] Redfern, 169.
[2] Cameron, 'The New Left in Britain', *The Night Battle*, 72–3.

force of the case that contemporary theologians have made, and with the inclusion of some fresh theological ideas, this is the essence of Redfern's argument.

It is obviously an argument at a high level of generality, and this is its characteristic weakness. What is obviously needed to complete it is a far more detailed account of what this 'closed' church—that is, the visible christian community—needs to be like, in relation to the world it has to serve. And this means evolving a strategy for changing the church from its present empirical form to something more adequate. But, by contrast with the concept of the church, which at least comes through as something known and experienced, Redfern's notion of socialism has hardly any edge at all. Socialism, according to him, is about

. . . eradicating all factors which divide society and mankind against themselves, whether these divisions are political, economic, educational, sexual, religious or any other. . . . This means that we are, willy nilly, committed in advance on all issues of segregation or unification.[1]

He tells us nothing about *how* to combat the evils that we have to face in capitalism. The vagueness continues when, instead of going on to say exactly what is required in terms of action for the emancipation of the workers and so defining socialism positively, Redfern can only do so negatively. He just tells us why we cannot subscribe to liberal democracy. There are three main reasons: (*a*) democracy is conceived too narrowly as a system for winning or maintaining a parliamentary majority. It is not recognised as existing for the formulation of policy and organisation of effort through-

[1] Redfern, 174.

out the range of daily activities; (*b*) it is a philosophy based on static, western presuppositions, lacks a sense of its own historical relativity, and is incapable of assimilating or coming to terms with the cultural forms and attitudes of the developing world; and (*c*) it is antichristian, because it takes itself to be the final culminating achievement of man as a political animal, and has no aspirations towards attempting to evolve

from the present élitist, merely elective, narrowly party-political level, to a more radically democratic, participative level which would hold good throughout economic and cultural as well as political institutions.[1]

Christianity demands such an evolution.

These criticisms of liberal democracy are part of the familiar currency of new left socialism, and can only be justly assessed and evaluated by reference to the detailed work that has been done to back them up with fact, evidence, and cogent argument. But even granted this, they remain theoretical, and do not explicitly acknowledge the difficulties involved in translating them into practice. This is not to suggest that writers of the catholic left are unaware of these difficulties, or that they have ignored them. *Slant* has published, for instance, a series of articles on the practice of industrial democracy through workers' control in Yugoslavia, Algeria, and elsewhere which bring out very clearly the problems and limitations of achieving such democracy.[2] But it is a valid criticism

[1] Redfern, 179.
[2] Ken Fleet, 'Workers' Control: the movement in Britain', *Slant* 11 (October–November 1966), 6–8; and Ian Clegg, 'Workers' control: a short history', *Slant* 11, 3–6; 'Workers' self-management in Algeria', *Slant* 12 (December 1966–January 1967), 16–19; and 'Self-management in Yugoslavia', *Slant* 13 (February–March 1967), 13–17.

of the catholic left that it has not so far provided enough analysis of this kind to establish its general position, or to rebut the charge of being solely 'engaged in a search for rhetorical solutions to tensions of an understandable, perhaps intolerable, but certainly idiosyncratic kind'.[1]

This is no doubt partly due to a lack of resources and manpower. It is also perhaps due to a feeling that the cases that most urgently need to be made are not those in which there is any special theological contribution to make: they are just the kind of cases that any socialist needs to make. But I think this feeling (if it exists) is a mistaken one. For if the demand for a revolutionary change within the church's own structure, as one necessary element in the total revolution that is required, is to be valid, then within this there are numerous analyses that must be made in Britain for a British catholic context. It would be wrong, of course, to suppose that none has been attempted. In the field of education, for instance, work of the right kind has been done by Joan Brothers, Monica Lawlor, and others;[2] and of course the symposia edited by Walter Stein on the nuclear problem are very significant contributions to that issue by any standards.[3] *Slant* itself has produced analyses of the right kind, too: for example, Charles Boxer's discussion of the problem of christianity within the community of the

[1] Raymond Williams, 'New Left Catholics', *New Black-friars* XLVIII, 558 (November 1966), 75.
[2] Joan Brothers, *Church and School*, Liverpool 1964; Monica Lawlor, *Out of this World*, London 1965; etc.
[3] Walter Stein (ed.), *Nuclear Weapons and Christian Conscience*, London 1961; and *Peace on Earth: the Way Ahead*, London 1966.

British army in Germany.[1] But, if what matters to the catholic left is that it should actually contribute to the moving of the church from its present condition to something new, this means doing more in producing the practical alternatives, evolving the strategy, and working on the evidence, as well as elaborating an intellectual critique. In a sense, the lack of any profound theology—other than that which it borrows from people (mostly foreigners) who often do not share a 'left' sympathy—is due to a lack of work on specific, hard 'cases'. For it is in the working out of these that a genuine theology takes root.

One important area in which such work is required is precisely where Williams's own concept of total secular redemption by a long revolution breaks down: that is to say, in the working out of the process by which mankind, whether with God or without him, is to overcome the fundamental paradoxes that I alluded to in the last chapter. Certainly, it is necessary first of all to show exactly how Williams's own argument fails at crucial points to make this transition, or how he fails to see the nature of the obstacle that has to be overcome. But Walter Stein has already done much of this in the articles referred to.[2]

This having been said, it is then necessary to turn to the details of any alternative that may be suggested. If the alternative is to be a transition that only God can help us to make, at Christ's second coming, how is this to be made relevant to our predicament here and now?

[1] Charles Boxer OP, 'The church as a community in the world': '1. A parish experience', *Slant* 13 (February–March 1967), 3–10; and '2. An interpretation', *Slant* 14 (April–May 1967), 21–4.
[2] See *n*. 1 on p. 57 above.

Obviously, as Redfern sees, it must be through a revolutionising of the church, seen as the sacrament and foreshadowing of the kingdom, that such a process must be mediated. This is important for two reasons. First, only a revolutionised church is capable of *being* such a sign in an adequate way; but secondly, the undertaking of this revolutionary action will be the one work that will convince the world that the church is the genuine sign of the hoped-for future. Only thus will it be able to bring men into it in full freedom and integrity, and so to do whatever can be done humanly to overcome the paradox itself.

But to revolutionise the church will be, necessarily, to revolutionise society. To be involved in the one long revolution will be to engage in the other. Detailed work is needed, then, on how the actual revolutionary action within the church is to proceed, and what the appropriate strategy is. For, essentially, the core of the argument is that the complete transition to a society in which the paradox is resolved is what is meant by the end of the world. It will mark the end of human struggle, its culmination in a victory that will simply give men the resolution of the tensions they experience and want, above all, to resolve. It will be a gift, then; a gratuitous, unexpected intervention into human history by a power which alone can envisage a human kind of life that is yet free from, and beyond, the paradox that human bodiliness, human conceptualisation, human sexuality entail. The human task is to prepare for this unexpected gift, by clearing away, in every direction, the obstacles that stand in the way of our seeing, clearly and unmistakably, the nature of the paradox that we are all involved in.

The political revolution is an action that will not, by itself, inaugurate the kingdom. Its function is to banish all the false dreams of the kingdom that men entertain—utopias and static perfect societies—by banishing the factors that lead men to those dreams— that is to say, by banishing all *religion* in the sense that Marx meant: partial interpretations of human life, based upon devotion to some element *within* existence (a 'God of the gaps' in human knowledge and control of the world), and offered in place of the one task to which men actually have a duty: their own freedom and its achievement. By banishing all false, religious dreams, including those dreamt by orthodox marxists about the socialist society itself, the revolution will leave clear and unambiguous the impossibility of man making the final transition by his own power alone. That is the whole purpose of the revolution, within the church and within society: to leave the field clear for the coming of Christ.

This sounds grandiose, and vague: and it is, until it is also understood that this is not a speculative idea, but a very particular commitment demanded of everyone here and now. It is not something that will just happen, at some distant future time. It is a concrete possibility to be worked for, which needs a detailed strategy, and even an immediate tactic. A working through of the priorities is necessary, and a sense of the length and complexity of the whole action. In the christian conception this working-out is not just a political matter, but also an ecclesiological one. Or rather, what is necessary is a recognition of the truth of the catholic left's contention that there can, in principle, be no absolute distinction between the two.

It is in finding a sense of the relevance of the total vision to the immediate need that the catholic left will discover itself, and make its unique contribution to the world's future.

2. The 'Culture and Liturgy' argument

I put the title of this section in quotation marks to indicate that, although one of the first formulations of this argument was given in my own earlier book of the same title, I have no proprietary rights to the argument itself, and others have since elaborated it in various ways—notably Terence Eagleton in *The New Left Church*. I think the fundamentals of the main argument still stand, though I think I would not now wish to state them in quite the same way as I did in 1963.

In a nutshell, the argument is simply this. It is an accepted part of modern theology that the liturgy is more than just the public act of the church. It is the act which makes the church to be a visible encounterable community in the world at all. That is to say, it is the only absolutely necessary way in which the church is visible. Everything which distinguishes christians from other people in the community—from dog-collars to special schools—is expendable. But the liturgy would have to remain. It is what the church must for ever continue to do, in some way or other, if it is to carry out the commands of its Lord : 'do this in commemoration of me'. Hence, the liturgy has the main role in building up the body of the faithful into a living community, the people of God. And also, it has the main role of making clear to those at present still outside the church, in the visible sense of the term, what the christian message of redemption is. That is to say, it mediates Christ to the world. It must do this in a way which will help people to accept it for themselves, freely and with full understanding.

All of this is, I think, generally accepted by christians, or at any rate by those with any concept of liturgy, whatever the implications they see in it for a social or political commitment. But it is also true that, for many christians, this theology of the liturgy involves something more: namely, a concept of how the liturgy is and ought to be related to the community outside. For it is not enough to say that the liturgy is about the building up of the christian body in the world without having some idea of what this means in terms of the actual state of the community of the church, as it actually exists at present, and of the state of the society in which it is placed as well. It is at this point that the argument engages the attention of the catholic left: for it follows from the comprehensive definition of politics the catholic left accepts that this problem is a political problem. Hence it is not enough to consider the liturgy as if it were just a christian, let alone just an ecclesiastical, affair. It poses a problem that can be tackled only on the understanding that the liturgy connects strictly christian values with all the values of the world beyond; and it does this, not at the level of ideas merely, but at the level of empirical social structures and lived political and social experience.

That is the general outline of the position. But it needs to be expanded—and has been expanded in various ways[1]—before it can bear the weight of a *left* position. The case for this is, no doubt, complex; but in the light of the preceding pages I think it can be reasonably abbreviated into the following considerations. The liturgy is a process of communication among persons who are gathered together into a community. The modes of this communication are various —words, gestures, music, the sharing of a common meal which is also a sharing in the life of Christ. Central to it, is the communication of Christ himself. But it is insufficient to think of this communication as consisting simply in the real presence of Christ in the physical elements. It is a presence to a community, and this is a community that has to be formed. It is not simply a datum taken from the world at large. The liturgical community has to be recalled, re-constituted, each celebration. This is especially true today, since the community of the liturgy is not, demographically speaking, simply the reappearance in the church of a community that in any case exists outside. It is a minority, finding itself in a world that is not only indifferent to it, but is in many ways structured on a totally different principle from that of the liturgy. For the liturgy is, primarily, a community of people radically equal before God and each other, and wholly committed to serving each other and finding their own

[1] See, for example, my own *Culture and Liturgy*, London 1963; and Terence Eagleton, *The New Left Church*, London 1966. Among the relevant articles are my own 'Theology and the New Left', *Slant* 1 (Spring 1964), 8–14; 'The Ministry of the Word', *New Blackfriars* XLVII, 545 (November 1965), 61–7; and 'Liturgy and Politics', *New Blackfriars* XLVII, 551 (April 1966); and Nicholas Lash, 'The Eucharist: Sacrament of Christ's Presence in the World', *New Blackfriars* XLVIII, 560 (January 1967), 172–85.

life in that dedication to common needs. Within this community there are, it is true, differences of function : but this is, theologically speaking—whatever may be said of the lived experience to the contrary—the only kind of difference that is legitimate.

Of course, such functional differences do entail, in a sense, a certain hierarchy of authority. For example a teacher, simply by virtue of his task, is 'superior' to his pupil in respect of the subject that he is teaching, and on which he is an authority. But even here—where the notion of superior and inferior relations is most obviously involved in the liturgy, since the liturgy is a teaching situation—a radical qualification has to be made. This is that the whole object of effective teaching is that it should produce eventually an equality between teacher and pupil in respect of the subject being communicated. This is what it means to say that one person has succeeded in teaching and the other in learning something.

Despite the hierarchy of function, then, the liturgy is radically egalitarian in its basic conception. And in this sense it is a scandal in the eyes of a world which is dedicated to quite other social structures—a world based on differences of 'intelligence', 'ability', 'attainment', 'class', 'wealth', 'status', 'rank', or even 'race' and 'religion'. Inevitably, then, the problem of the liturgy is a problem of creating the christian community, in a condition of tension with the world. That is, quite clearly and obviously, a political problem. For it is a question of achieving a radically egalitarian society, with nothing but functional differentiation within it, against the grain of what is experienced elsewhere. This is the basic reason why a genuine understanding of the theology of liturgy must involve, in a general sense, a socialist commitment. For, as I have insisted, this egalitarianism is what socialism is about. Of course, to say that and then leave it there is grossly inadequate. In the first place, socialism as an aspiration towards an egalitarian society is by no means generally understood or accepted. In practice, socialism is as likely in our society to be advocated for reasons of expediency, or efficiency, as for reasons of an ethical nature.

Furthermore, it is by no means the case that those who, in a loose sense, think of themselves as socialist necessarily want an egalitarian society. Finally, even if it is accepted—as it is by the new left—that this *is* what socialism is about, a detailed argument has to be maintained to show that equality does not mean a drab uniformity. It has to be maintained and shown that there are no absolute natural obstacles to human equality, built into the very constitution of men. That is to say, all those elements which are said to count against human equality have to be shown to be either contingent upon a certain context or capable of being accommodated within a concept of *functional* differences that does not entail permanent inequalities of an objectionable, non-functional kind. This necessary argument involves perpetual struggle because the emotional and other forces against it are so strong. And even if it is accepted as a valid argument, to propound it is only the beginning. It has to be accepted widely enough to be acted upon; and this is where the real battle, the genuine political engagement, begins. These considerations mean that, even when an understanding of the nature of the liturgy is available, the commitment to socialism that follows is one that requires a profound dedication to detailed work, persistence, rationality and endurance.

A further consideration that must be noted is that what the liturgy is trying to communicate is a body of ideas, feelings, sensibilities, and historical insights that, taken together, constitute a very formidable constellation. In fact, what is to be achieved is nothing other than a complete christian education, which again takes place against the grain of the external society. To communicate Christ is to communicate him as a man, with a history and a culture that is an integral part of himself. It is the christian demand, furthermore, that this communication can, and should, be offered affectively to all men, of every kind. What this really means, then, is that it is an integral element of christian belief that this communication of a whole culture—a culture which is in many ways strange, complex and difficult to grasp for those not born into it—can be made, without entailing any insuperable demands on the ordinary person. And to say this is, of course, to rate the capacities of the ordinary person very highly—far more highly than is done in the world at large. For, outside the limits of a fairly radical socialist circle, it is a plain fact that such an undertaking is generally believed to be an educational impossibility, partly because it is too complex and partly because the ordinary person is held to be imaginatively incapable of understanding and absorbing the material. It is historically the case, that the belief in the capacity of the ordinary person—under the most favourable conditions no doubt—to achieve this kind of educational profundity is a characteristic mark of the left. Not only has most of the work on the details of the case been done by the left: the left alone has a real stake in making it come true.

At this point a common feeling, which could be elevated to the status of a quasi-theological argument, against this whole thesis needs to be considered. It is that, in thinking of the liturgy as a communication between men, in a culturally determined setting, God's power of enlightening the human heart is being left out of account. In other words, it might be argued that what men themselves lack in basic intellectual, imaginative, and emotional capacity for understanding God's revelation in Christ, God himself will 'make up'. And further, it might be said that this is the whole object of the liturgy—not to communicate a human message, in a human way, but to communicate God's message, in a divine way. This divine way would presumably somehow bypass the inherent difficulties of educating the ordinary person into a complex high culture of a strange and alien kind. It would be done by bypassing the ordinary processes of hearing and learning, and use instead the spiritual element of man as a medium for the infusion of the message directly. For it is said that the liturgy is prayer rather than education. Thus it might be possible to hold that the liturgy does not entail radical social commitment to an egalitarian society, with all that this implies, but rather the opposite. It emphasises that, despite the intrinsic differences of capacity, attainment, and status that hold in the world—and, it might be further argued, *ought* to be maintained—the christian liturgy contradicts them, by holding up for view an ideal (to be attained hereafter, but not sought in this world) which has its appeal precisely because it is a challenge to the world as it is. And for this challenge to be maintained, of course, the world must remain as it substantially is —as the opposite pole of a christian dialectic with an evil world.

The answer to this concept is at once theological and moral. Theologically, the concept is a misreading of the idea of the sacrament. It undermines the sacramental idea, which is that the communication of Christ comes *through*, not *in spite of*, human capacities. The greater these capacities are, the greater the communication that can be achieved, and the more intelligible and acceptable the 'sign' that the sacramental action offers of the presence of Christ in the world. Of course, it is not that human capacities are to be measured merely by the standards of the educational establishment. I am not suggesting that the capacity of the ordinary person to understand and receive the message of Christ is somehow measurable by such crude, and often loaded, criteria as (say) a pass in the eleven-plus examination. What I mean by the capacity of people to understand is something much more genuinely educational than anything such tests measure. Yet, at the same time it would be wrong to suppose that there is no relation to be understood even here. To speak of christian education as if it were in no sense at all concerned with such standards, or their replacement by others that are less unfair and restrictive, would be to miss the hard kernel of the political commitment that, I am arguing, the whole thesis of the catholic left involves. There *is* a connection between (say) the idea of the liturgy as a communication of Christ, and the establishment of comprehensive schools. For these are designed to be the means for the maximum, genuine education of free people in a society released from the anti-christian, artificial differences that the prevailing system endorses, and in which men's capacities are fully stretched in all directions—academic, emotional, artistic, and the rest. (To put the claim so crudely as this is, of course, grossly inadequate by itself. But the work on this particular issue has largely been done, and is available for anyone open to rational persuasion to examine for himself. The new left can take its fair share of credit for this fact.)

That is the core of the case on the 'culture and liturgy' front. It has implications of very many kinds. In one sense, it takes us towards the dismantling of the church as a quasi-political structure, and begins to give us a bearing on the problem of what kind of structure needs to be put in its place. But the detailed strategy has yet to be worked out. In another sense it leads towards a recognition that, contrary to what many liturgical thinkers of an older generation have thought, there is no sense and no good in the idea of retreating to a medieval concept of the community permanently centred upon just one locality for its sustenance. The liturgy in modern, urban conditions cannot be conducted on any other than the 'service-station' basis. That is to say, it must be provided by a church which is felt and experienced as a universal presence, not centred on the local community (which, effectively, scarcely exists in the relevant sense). People will call in at the liturgy wherever they happen to be, and will have to be gathered into the community from that point. The allegiance will be to a church felt as the sacrament of mankind's total unity, rather than as the sacrament of the unity of a particular local, professional, or other kind of group. This, by itself, involves radical implications for the structure and operation of the church itself in its institutional role.

But even at this point a sense of unreality breaks in. What immediate connections does such a theory of the liturgy, and such a demand, have for the ordinary christian, in his ordinary liturgical experience? The very size and scope of the claim puts it at a distance from the ordinary level, so that nothing seems to be changeable in the relevant way. Where, it has to be asked, are we to *start*? And is it not a fact that it is only possible to dream of the required changes if one is already alienated from this ordinary life by a kind of intellectual withdrawal from reality? In a sense, of course, this is where faith comes in. We have to try to see, with the eyes of faith, what we are unable to see in ordinary terms, because in ordinary terms what we see is something altogether different, and seemingly inadequate to bear the strain to be put on it. But we must not use the idea of faith to distract us from the reality of this situation. Faith is not a substitute for detailed strategy and action, but only a basis for working it out.

It is at this point, once more, that the catholic left has not, yet, made any very significant mark.[1] Perhaps more has been done, for instance, by groups actively engaged in trying to alter the whole basis of the education of the clergy, by bringing them into closer contact with the cultural life of the modern world in the uni-

[1] One significant exception to this generalisation is the two-part article by Charles Boxer already cited (see *n.* 1 on p. 78 above), in which he attempts to show that it is still the parish that should be the focus of attention and revolution.

versities, than by the catholic left as such. The sense of remoteness from actualities that even the 'culture and liturgy' argument still suffers from is important, not only because this is a serious weakness in itself, but also because it creates a 'credibility gap' that urgently requires filling. This is not just a gap that those not of the catholic left, however sympathetic, often feel; it is also a gap that the left itself feels, and ought to feel perhaps more acutely. For, as Martin Green has rightly said,[1] there is a danger of an inward corruption in a group which spends its energies calling for, and waiting for, a revolution that is not likely to happen yet, and which meanwhile seems to find it possible to live happily and comfortably in the unrevolutionised situation.

3. Morality and revolution

The main point that needs to be made on this topic has already been outlined (see p. 72 above). Moral intransigence is necessary as a stimulus to changing an evil situation, and not just tolerating it, making the best of it. There are a number of difficulties however, in working out this part of the catholic left case. One is that, when one considers the argument as it applies to specific instances, the clarity and force of the general point seem to melt away. Only in the case of nuclear weapons has the case been clearly and thoroughly maintained. This is no doubt largely due to the fact that it is a natural and obvious part of a 'left' approach. Where moral intransigence *seems* to imply a

[1] Martin Green, 'Comment', *New Blackfriars* XLVIII, 557 (October 1966), 3–6.

reactionary, rather than a revolutionary, attitude—as, it must be confessed it very often does (e.g, in the abortion controversy)—the intransigence is hard to maintain. This is a disturbing situation, and it needs examining. A second, linked difficulty is that in this case, as in previous cases examined, the familiar paradox—that is, a need for several incompatible conceptual frameworks—reappears and must be taken into account.

The two conceptual frameworks in question here are those of morality as 'love' and morality as 'law'. The accusation that the catholic left thinker makes against the 'new morality', insofar as the latter claims to base itself upon the primacy of love alone in morality, is that it makes love a matter of purely interior disposition, divorced from any overt, detectable behaviour.[1] The new moralist usually says this, when pushed to a limit, because he insists that there is no kind of outward action that is always and necessarily wrong irrespective of circumstances. He starts from the principle that the only act that is wrong is an act done without love. Sometimes he goes on to argue that, provided that an action is undertaken with love, it is morally virtuous—even, perhaps, an act of mass-killing like the dropping of the Hiroshima atom-bomb.

A 'love' morality conceived on such a basis is naturally conservative. As long as you have love 'in your heart', it seems to imply, it is not logically necessary to *act* in a loving way by (say) changing the whole situation. That most 'new moralists' would not, them-

[1] This point has been best made by Herbert McCabe OP, in an article (*Commonweal*, 14 January 1966) in which he was disputing with Joseph Fletcher on the subject of the 'new morality'.

selves, accept this conclusion in practice is no answer to the objection that is being raised against it as a matter of moral *theory*. All the same, if this is a valid point against a certain way of moralising—a way which tries to interpret the moral situation wholly in terms of a single conceptual framework—there are equally difficult problems facing the moralist who stands upon 'law', even if he does so in a non-legalistic way. To say that there are some kinds of act which are invariably wrong implies that it is always possible to describe such kinds of behaviour in such a way that their wickedness is evident. (This does not mean, of course, that it is easy to provide such a description, or that the description will be a simple one.) And to say this is to erect a notion of moral *law* or standard, which is not necessarily a law that is imposed from above. Nor does the view deny that only loving behaviour is good. It simply says that the very notion of love, because it can only make sense in terms of loving *behaviour*, implies that it is possible to distinguish, according to some principle, loving behaviour from unloving behaviour—otherwise the whole point of the assertion that only loving behaviour is good would vanish. We would not be able to apply it in practice, by making proper moral choices between possible ways of behaving.

But the position involves more than this. It suggests that this law, according to which one can distinguish loving from unloving behaviour, is necessary for mankind. For moral law is simply an expression of what man's needs are, and hence of what kinds of behaviour he must avoid if he is to satisfy those needs. Somehow, it is being argued, we *know* that only loving behaviour does us any good. But this is a useless belief unless we can show how it works in practice. The *logic* of the idea of moral law may be that it is designed to tell us what to avoid in order to do good to ourselves. (That is, it is not designed to tell us what God wants, but rather what we need ourselves.) But unless this logic is displayed somehow, it does not take us very far. The next step then has to be some kind of attempt to show that only by keeping to a moral law can social life be maintained, and what kind of law this must be. Now it is not inconceivable that a purely philosophical argument could be adduced for this. (The argument for a natural law put forward by Aquinas, for example, was just such a case.) But for us, in our modern world, such a formalistic attempt is certain to fail. More promising perhaps is an attempt to show imaginatively, in fictional worlds, how moral law works in practice in concrete particular circumstances. For we are familiar with the process by which, in the novel or the drama, an imagined world is related to the real world and made significant for that reason. The aesthetic and moral validity that we see in the fictional world, as displayed by an author with integrity and insight, is necessarily a proof of the validity of the same, or at any rate a similar, conception in real terms.

When such an examination of fictional worlds is attempted, I think the paradox of the competing incompatible frameworks soon emerges. One quickly sees—in the case of a book like Conrad's *Lord Jim*, for instance—how this paradox expresses itself in the concrete case. Conrad, the seafaring man of discipline and honour, and absolute moral standards, sees that men are ineradicably social. He accepts, too, that the structure of any society worthy of the name—and the seafaring community is, in this sense, a microcosm of the real world—must rest upon a code of conduct which consists of unimpeachable fiats addressed imperiously and without qualification to every man. Society cannot subsist, Conrad tries to show—and our response to his work is the measure of how far we feel we must agree with him—on a mere rule-of-thumb basis. To suggest that, in a critical dilemma, it may be actually virtuous to break the code that exists for the sake of man's own social being, is simply irrational. Yet, at the same time, it is clear that the presence of such a code is liable, at times of stress and moral agony, to break the man who tries to keep it (this is what happens to Captain Brierly in *Lord Jim*) and to break the man who betrays it (Jim himself). And this is true even when the breach of the code that is made is committed for 'love', even love of the most complete and genuine kind. Thus the morality of the code and the morality of 'love'—for love seems of its very nature to outrun all limits and codes, and to make no exception to the field of its operation—are in collision with each other in this novel. The two conceptual frameworks collide, in a tension that exists precisely because, from both sides, the basic needs and aspirations of men are being respected and endorsed.

To accept this tension is, of course, to accept tragedy. Conrad is pessimistic in this sense. 'This man's sufferings appal me because they are necessary.' Such acceptance is anti-revolutionary, for it admits that here is a situation which could not have been different.

Now we may try to eliminate the tension, in a revolutionary way, by accepting the validity of the code, and then insisting on the need to change the circumstances that brought the tragedy about. Or we may try to do it in a reformist way, by disregarding the code, and holding on to the morality of love at all costs, including the cost of accepting the situation and trying to make something of it. This is the problem of a moral intransigence that tries to be revolutionary. It will either eliminate a necessary tension in life, by interpreting all moral problems in terms of a single conceptual framework, that of the moral law, or it will betray the revolution by allowing the intransigence at certain crucial points to be relaxed for the sake of 'love'. The problem can be partly overcome, by showing that very often what looks like a concession to 'love' in the largest sense is, in fact, just a concession to some *private* urge which is not, really, love at all. The insistence that love is a behaviour in the public world, which is therefore manifestly *for others*, is part of a whole social well-being, not the satisfaction of a purely private need—is useful in separating out the genuine dilemma from the specious one.

But this is not enough to solve all the cases. The paradox can arise between problems within a wholly public, social world. Again, the insistence by catholic left writers that this social world can not be described in wholly 'objective' terms, as though the moralist himself were outside it, surveying and judging it but not being personally involved, is important. It protects the left from any tendency to write off personal difficulties and sensibilities as being of no absolute consequence. But these precautions only clarify the problem, by clearing away the false appearances of paradox:

they do not solve the paradox itself. Indeed, as I have already argued, humanly speaking the paradox is unavoidable. What matters is to see to it that only the genuine paradox is left to be faced.

But perhaps the paradox in its absolutely unambiguous form is never encountered, not because it does not exist, but because human organisation is always marred by ignorance, stupidity, and fear. Possibly there is no point in the real world at which a man has to face an absolute stark moral choice between keeping the law and behaving lovingly: not because there is no conflict in principle between the two, but because he can never be absolutely sure that the conflict is not, partly, due to his own or society's failure.

4. Conclusion

The whole purpose of the genuine christian revolution, as I understand it, is to bring man to the point where he has to face himself freely and alone with his own choice. The moment at which all the human obstacles and illusions and evasions have been cleared away, and the choice becomes absolutely stark, will be the point at which history ends and the kingdom of God begins. That is to say, it will not be a moment *through* which man has to live, and which offers a world of freedom which is exercisable only within an irrational order, where 'love' and 'law' become irreconcilable. It will be the moment at which the world has to be wholly transfigured by God, because it has to become a new world, in which that conflict is left behind altogether. Tragedy and revolution are, in such a conception, held together but in a tension. Tragedy *is* inevitable, because all history (as distinct from the life of man in the kingdom which comes after history is ended) contains the seeds of tragedy. But revolution is necessary because it is a moral imperative for man, by himself, to try to eliminate those seeds of tragedy. The fact that, in the end, the job has to be finished by a power greater than his own does not in the least excuse him from persisting in that effort. The moral position of the catholic left must, I think, rest in an acknowledgement of this revolutionary perspective.

I want to suggest, then, at this point, a task for the catholic left. I have already indicated some kinds of intellectual work that, I think, it urgently needs to do, in evolving a detailed strategy for the revolutionising of the church, and its relation to the world. This certainly means making the thorough, tough analyses and cases that Raymond Williams has demanded, along the whole front that extends between reform and revolution; and it means, too, giving priorities and seeing connections between these areas. But there is also a need for a different kind of work. I may best suggest what I mean by referring to the idea of man eliminating the seeds of tragedy *by himself*—by which I mean, precisely, without the help of any external power that is not his own. But this does not mean that God is not to be reckoned with here. It means recognising God as having made himself over to man completely, having put himself into man's hands to be used in a human way. This is the meaning of the incarnation: a surrendering of God into man's power, and thereby giving man a power he otherwise could not possess.

Now such a notion of God is, in many ways, the exact opposite of the God christians have been brought up to believe in. Familiarly, that is to say, God is experienced as a person apart from ourselves, who has his own power in himself, but who on occasions— perhaps when the sacraments are being 'administered', perhaps when a tragedy is threatened but does not come about, perhaps when men are praying, or making love—gives us a small amount of that power, or 'grace', to help us out. This is, in fact, the christian God as men usually experience him in the church as it presently exists, or as men usually reject him when they reject the church. But it is not the God that christianity, as such, offers us. Nor is it a God that any self-respecting person in the modern world can accept. It is not the God that Christ reveals to us in his self-surrender to men in life, death, and resurrection.

The God of christianity is one who has abandoned us to our own world, and who has asked us to make what we can of it by ourselves. This is the authentic christian God. And it is extremely significant that it is not the church, as an institution, which has made this clear to modern men. It is rather those thinkers who, having seen the kind of god the church offers, have turned away, and through that very action have understood that we have to live in a world abandoned by that God. Now when this is said by one christian to another—at least, to one who is familiar with modern theology—it will not seem particularly surprising. But it does seem completely surprising and shocking to the christian who is not well up in that theology. And—what is more important still—it is equally shocking to the non-christian who thinks that what he has rejected *is* christianity itself. For he finds that the very thing he rejected in christianity—and rightly—is now being rejected by the christians them-selves, and (what is worse) his agnosticism is now being paraded by them as the *authentic* christianity. Faced by such an apparent band-waggoning hypocrisy by the christian, he is even more sickened than before. He could respect the other, old-fashioned christianity, even if he disagreed with it. But this version cannot even be respected. For it is nothing but a piece of gigantic self-deception being displayed as the one true gospel of salvation for all!

There is only one way of overcoming this perfectly genuine response, whether it is made by an old-style christian or a non-christian. What is required is a detailed study of the process, from the human, or cul-tural end, by which the old God—the 'God of the gaps'—has been abandoned, and the new God—the God of the incarnation—has replaced him. We need this history for two reasons. As christians we need it because we have to relate our understanding of the God of the incarnation to the kind of feelings and re-sponses which have kept the God of the gaps in busi-ness for so long after he had become obsolete. We need to see what has actually happened, in human culture, in this slow process of displacement. Without this 'cultural history of God' we cannot understand the meaning of our own belief. But it is needed also in order to make this God of the incarnation intelligible intellectually and emotionally to others as well. We need to show how it is that the *concept* of God—which, unlike God 'as he is in himself' is always shaped by our particular needs at a particular place and time in human history—has changed, and in what particular ways. If the concept of the God of the gaps was once a relevant concept, this was because of the cultural needs of the time. If the God of the incarnation is needed now, it is because of our own cultural needs.

But we cannot leave the matter there. Human cultural needs are continually changing, and the concept of God changes accordingly. Even the God of the gaps is not a static idea, but has itself changed radically. The God who, for the Hebrews, ruled the Jews but not, at any rate so vigilantly, the gentiles, and whose voice was the thunder and whose power was the quenchless fire, was a God specially associated with particular aspects of the world. It was through those aspects that he manifested himself. Even if, in theory, he was ruler of all, in concrete experience this was how he appeared and acted. He was a God of the gaps in the sense that it was particularly where men's own control and knowledge ended that God's power began. But for the eighteenth-century deists, say, God was not needed in that kind of role any more. He was not even needed to fill in the one gap left in the Newtonian world-picture—Laplace had plugged even that. God was now merely the person who had wound the world-mechanism up in the first place, and given it the 'push' that set it in perpetual motion.

Here a radically different concept of God related to a radically different kind of gap. But today, the whole idea of a God of any kind of gap is implausible, at any rate in an advanced industrial culture. It is only at moments of semi-hypocritical failure that we think of God as helping us, directly by his own power, out of a jam. The God we need to envisage is not a God of any particular gaps, but rather a God who is present throughout the one, pervasive discontinuity that we have now discovered: namely, the discontinuity between the whole of the natural world (the world of the scientific humanist conceptual framework) and the human world (the world of the socialist-humanist conceptual framework). I have tried to suggest how this discontinuity emerges at certain kinds of point in our ordinary experience. But these are only outcroppings of a pervasive, universal discontinuity that we must recognise if we are to survive at all. Without making this recognition, we shall soon submerge ourselves in a morass of naturalism, an inert world of human objects, from which we may never extricate ourselves. The God of the incarnation is a God who lives in that discontinuity and makes it tolerable.

Now, as I have said, it is one of the merits of the new left to have been more sharply aware than most other people of the extent and nature of this discontinuity. It would be absurd to credit them with having found it. But at any rate, within the British cultural climate, dominated as it is by quite different assumptions, they have preserved and developed this concept in a fruitful way. That they have not been able to deal with it adequately—precisely because they have not accepted any God, not even the God of the incarnation—I have tried to make clear. But they have done more than most people to think about it. What is now needed, to make full use of this recognition, is of course to fill out the very shadowy concept of the God of the incarnation (shadowy for us, that is, in relation to our cultural needs). But this cannot be done without a sense of the history that has led up to it. We need to know the detailed history of this concept, over (say) the last fifty years, as evidenced in (for example) the literature and the other concept-forming activities of our culture. The literature would, of course, be very largely the literature of atheism—the literature of a world abandoned by any God that men brought up in the familiar christian perspective can believe in. What such a study might reveal is how it feels, in this epoch, to be thus abandoned, and what kind of God might be put in its place.[1]

---

[1] For a philosophical discussion of this theme, Leslie Dewart's important book *The Future of Belief* (London 1967) would certainly be a significant starting point. See my review article in *New Blackfriars* XLVIII, 565 (June 1967) 468–78, for a discussion of this book in the context of the above remarks.

4
The continuing debate

The purpose of this final chapter is to give the reader
some idea of the debate that has been carried on about
the aims and methods of the catholic left in Britain in
the last few years. It takes the form of extracts from
some of the more representative and serious articles
that have been devoted to the subject, connected by
my own commentary. It would be a mistake to suppose that this selection is comprehensive, but my
object has been to indicate some of the main points
around which argument has centred, and the characteristic lines of thought that have emerged.

I begin with an article by Michael Dummett entitled
'How Corrupt is the Church?' and published in August 1965.[1] This article represents the kind of 'progressive' catholic thinking that the left has tended to
stigmatise as 'liberal' in a derogatory sense. That is to
say, while Dummett admits the validity of many points

[1] Michael Dummett, 'How Corrupt is the Church?', *New
Blackfriars* XLVI, 542 (August 1965), 619–28. The article has
been reprinted in *The Purification of the Church: five comments from New Blackfriars*, ed. Ian Hislop OP, London 1967,
27–39.

that the left makes concerning weaknesses and failures of the church, it might be said that he fails to see their full implications in political terms. Dummett makes a political diagnosis, but fails to draw the appropriate political conclusion.

The article begins by admitting that the church can be corrupt, and that we are now emerging from a period of profound corruption—not of the obvious kind, perhaps ('simony at the papal court, or pluralist-bishops, or priests with concubines and children'), but nevertheless deeply damaging. One sign of this corruption has been the inability of the church—evidenced at the Vatican council—to do more than fumble with the two most pressing practical moral issues that face it: contraception, and nuclear war. (The article, of course, was written before the council ended.) This evasion is evidence of a failure to dig deep enough, or to admit the full evil of what has been done in the past. This is particularly true of the church's past weakness in the field of anti-semitism, in its failure to resist Hitler, and in the failure to prevent the use of nuclear weapons during the second world war. There is still no real recognition of how corrupting the failure to take a clear stand on these issues has been in the life of the church. Dummett goes on:

It is one thing to recognize from the symptoms that the Church must be corrupt: it is another to diagnose in what that corruption consists. I am going to mention one thing which seems to me a defect of the gravest kind: there may well be others to which I am blind. The point I am going to make is one that is fairly familiar, at least as applied to parishes: but, I do not think that people have generally appreciated the gravity of the matter. The fact is this: that, while many inside the Church are living, or trying to live, Christian lives as individuals, the Church, *as a body*, has not been leading a Christian life at all. In our time we have come to realize more forcefully that the Mass is the supreme act *of a community*, and an expression of charity between the members of that community. But this realization is hollow when what is symbolized in this corporate act simply does not exist in reality. Neither the parish, nor the Church as a whole, is a community at all, in the sense in which a village, or a section of a city, or even an Oxford college, forms a community. The Church is at present merely a *religious* association: an organization to which those can belong who accept certain religious views, which exists solely to supply to its members what will fulfil their strictly religious needs. We do not know one another, we do not care for one another, and we have nothing in common with one another save our acceptance of certain religious tenets.

This is grossly wrong. We have before us all the time the pattern of the earliest Christian community, described in the Acts and in the Epistles: and we know that it constituted a society which undertook to care for its members. Indeed, it did not tolerate parasites (' if a man will not work, so neither let him eat'): but it accepted the responsibility to support and help its less fortunate members, the poor, the widows and the orphans. And this not only *within* each local church: when one particular church was in trouble as a whole, the other church provided relief. This pattern is so clearly laid down for us in Scripture, that it is a matter of bewilderment that we should ever have dared to depart from it. It ought to be taken for granted that a Catholic parish is a society of people who look after one another: acceptance of responsibility for the welfare of other members of the community ought to be a known condition of becoming a Catholic. In any parish, there are always many struggling with hardship: the poor, the out of work, the sick, the crippled, the very old: those with many children, those with sick or mentally defective children, those who have to take care of the old or the crippled or the ill. And in any parish, there are also those who are more fortunate, and it should be accepted without question, as being simply a part of what it is to be a Catholic, that the latter should help the former. But we do not even undertake to help the less fortunate in the performance of their strictly religious duties: there are many so hampered by their domestic obligations that, year after year, they are unable to participate in the great liturgical celebrations, and able to attend ordinary Sunday Mass only fitfully. I say that in every parish there are those who are more fortunate: for even if everyone suffers from misfortune, those who are unfortunate in one way may be fortunate in another; those oppressed by poverty may have time to spare for others, those who have no time may have money or room in their houses. But, if we accepted these ideas as an ordinary part of Catholic life, we should see to it that, as far as possible, a parish did represent a cross-section of the social structure: we should so draw the parish boundaries that every parish included some who were well off as well as some who were poor; whereas now, very often, the parish is neatly devised to include only members of a single social class.

Of course, I am not denying that charitable works have constantly been a standard part of Catholic life, for instance by such bodies as the Society of St. Vincent de Paul. But such works have been thought to be a special vocation of a minority, rather than a normal part of the obligation which any Catholic accepts; and it has been a matter of dispensing charity to a few hard cases. A comparatively well off mother, struggling with seven children, or a respectable middle-aged spinster, tied to an aged and bed-ridden father, does not want, and does not think she ought, to become a 'case' on an S.V.P. list: whereas, if it were taken for granted that a Catholic parish is a community in which we *all* help *one another*, each giving what he is capable of, the atmosphere would be quite different, and no-one would be embarrassed or affronted at being offered help.

This cannot be confined to the parish level: sometimes help will be needed which simply cannot be provided by the resources of the parish. It ought to be universally accepted that the Church, as a community, has the obligation to assure, so far as is humanly possible, tolerable conditions of life to her members. There is much to quarrel with in Dr. Biezanek's book: but one thing in it which, in my view, is wholly justified is her complaint that when, by trying to live in accordance with what she then believed, and had been told, were the requirements of Christian morality, she was faced with the loss of her job, the dispersal of her children, and the breakdown of her health, the Church as a body simply refused to acknowledge the responsibility of saving her from these disasters. It seems clear to me that, if we lived *as a Christian body*, rather than as a number of individual Christians who happen to be present in the same building for worship periodically, we should have ample resources with which to save any of our members from being driven into such a state, and that we ought therefore, as a body, to accept it as our duty to do so.

If you reflect for a moment on how things would be if this doctrine had been accepted and put into practice, you will see how many, many evils in the Church, great and small, would have been avoided. There might have been, as there is now, a doubt raised within the Church about the correctness of the traditional teaching on contraception: but it is unthinkable that those who raised it would have done so in the spirit of bitter resentment that is now so evident, if all along those who were burdened with large families received the constant assistance of their fellow-Catholics in the back-breaking task of coping with them. We complain of the cruel attacks that are made on us from outside on this issue: but, if things had been as I am saying that they ought to be, who would have had the face to criticize us for heartlessness? Take, again, the scandal of wealthy or upper-class Catholics who have continued, with no awareness of inconsistency, to adopt towards Catholics of lower social class the attitude of aloofness and superiority standard in their society. This was possible only against the background of a Church that existed for a specifically *religious* purpose: such attitudes would simply have broken down if these people had had, as an ordinary part of their duties, to mind the children or scrub the floors of their poorer fellow-Christians; and the same goes for the shocking expressions by Catholics of racial prejudice, on the letter page of the *Catholic Herald*, as well as in South Africa or Louisiana. All I am saying amounts to this: that Christians ought to be an example to the world of Christian charity; and they palpably are not. Sometimes we repeat to ourselves the words, 'See how these Christians love one another': ought we not to ask ourselves, 'How long is it since these words could be uttered without mockery?'[1]

Terry Eagleton's reply to this analysis, published in the following October, is characteristic of the kind of argument that the catholic left most typically deploys:

Mr Dummett's article . . . strikes me as showing a serious failure at certain points to press a real concern with renewal through to its full conclusions. Mr Dummett remarks, very rightly, that we have lost a sense of community as a Church, and he goes on to suggest that one way in which this can be regained is by a reorganiza-

[1] Dummett, 626–8 (*Purification of the Church*, 36–9).

tion of the parish. If we accepted the idea of community in parish life, he says, 'we should see to it that, as far as possible, a parish did represent a cross-section of the social structure: we should so draw the parish boundaries that every parish included some who were well off as well as some who were poor; whereas now, very often, the parish is neatly divided to include only members of a single social class'.

This is in fact a very reactionary statement, not progressive at all. For in trying helpfully to re-organize existing structures to create a better sense of community, Mr Dummett is in fact merely accepting and reinforcing a whole social *status quo*: he presumes without questioning the fact that society will be composed inevitably of rich and poor, different social classes, and takes this as a framework within which his progressive ideas operate; whereas in fact, of course, the proposition that in any good society the present social and economic divisions between men will continue to exist is very arguable indeed. It is this failure to see Christian and social structures in constant inter-relation which is so marked in progressive thinking (I am not by the way implying that Mr Dummett is generally a 'progressive' since he has doubts about the term, only that this attitude is typical of progressive thinking). The progressive does not only accept the *status quo* and then work within it: he may well, as Mr Dummett does here, actually sharpen the existing situation by the changes he proposes. Changes in Christian structures which seem good when the Church is seen in isolation from society can be actively harmful when looked at in a whole social context. In the same article, Mr Dummett makes the point that the parish ought to be a genuine community of mutual help and welfare: he says it always contains many suffering hardship, 'the poor, the out of work, the sick, the crippled, the very old . . .' But what needs to be pointed out here is that social structures for dealing with this hardship already exist (extremely inadequately, of course), and the real centre of Christian commitment, surely, is engaged in the work of creating and sustaining these common structures —the Church in the world—rather than the creation of a substitute welfare State within the parish which can patch and repair human damage and thereby (as in the last century) take pressure off the society which is supposed to be doing this itself in the first place. Such a parish would be humane and progressive, but it could well prove a new type of progressive ghetto, concerned with *Catholic* welfare and community rather than just human community. To renew an existing institution like the parish, making it into an effective community with its own welfare services and workers and activities, may actually weaken and confuse an overall social condition by diverting Christian energies from where they should really be focused: on the work of creating, not a community within a society, but simply a good, communal society. The conservative wants to keep given structures more or less as they are; the liberal wants to make them work more efficiently and humanely; the radical believes that in the case of certain structures no real change can be made short of total re-thinking. The question of whether the parish is itself the best unit is a valid one, and needs to be asked before we start wondering how to make it work: divisions of the Church which are based on historically outdated divisions of society, and which tend to duplicate social activities and thus create a new kind of enclosure, may well be less valuable than structures working inside and along with social institutions: centred on industry, for instance. The progressive's criticism works too much within an uncritical acceptance of given datum: he lacks the ability to distance himself to the point where he can ask the basic questions, those obvious to the non-Catholic observer. If we begin at a point short of the observer's starting-point, taking the basic facts for granted, we may simply undercut his confidence that what we are engaged on has living relevance to himself: his concern falls as a result from personal concern to academic interest.[1]

Dummett replied to this criticism in the December 1965 issue of *New Blackfriars*. He repudiated the suggestion that he thought class and social divisions of the kind at present operative in Britain were immutable, or that he approved of them. His concern, however, was practical; what should the christian do in a world where, for the time being, these problems exist? To rely solely on the welfare state for the amelioration of suffering was not enough—it was too impersonal to deal completely with human needs. The parish, as a community in which people of all classes and occupations mixed together and knew each other, was a useful instrument for this purpose—at least until something better could be envisaged. However, these points of disagreement, according to Dummett, were only symptomatic of a deeper disagreement about fundamental principle:

If I understand him, Mr Eagleton sees the Church primarily as a divinely ordained instrument for the transformation—even before the conversion—of the whole of human society; a Christian equivalent of the Communist Party (the spearhead of the revolution), or perhaps, if I may so express it, a kind of international pressure group. I do not see it in this way. Of course, the Church must work on the world, as the leaven in the lump: but I think

[1] Terry Eagleton, 'The Language of Renewal', *New Blackfriars* XLVII, 544 (October 1965), 21–3.

her primary task must be, not to transform secular society, but to create a better one within it. The Church *must* always 'stand over against the world': she ought to be able to achieve, within her own life as a community, the realisation of those ideals of mutual love, of sharing with and helping one another, which are necessarily, I think, unattainable for society as a whole (at least, for unconverted society), and present them to the world as an example, a goal and a reproach. Some will accuse me of being idealistic in supposing that, after the first three centuries, Christians can any more attain this: but surely our baptism should be capable of making a more visible difference than there is now between our ways and those of the society around us which has still to be redeemed. This fundamental disagreement between us, which is the core of Mr Eagleton's distinction between progressives and radicals, is one which must interest a number of people, and I hope others may have some light to throw upon it.[1]

The argument between Dummett and Eagleton provoked Bernard Bergonzi to contribute a note on the subject the following March (1966), which took the debate a little further:

Should we not be careful to avoid the kind of implicitly totalitarian attitude that gives supreme importance to the political order at the expense of every other kind of

[1] Michael Dummett, 'Church and World: Mr Dummett Replies', *New Blackfriars* XLVII, 546 (December 1965), 139–40. The hope expressed in Dummett's last sentence has been most notably fulfilled by the two-part article of Charles Boxer's in *Slant* 13 and 14 already cited (see *n.* 1 on p. 78 above). Boxer has taken this debate between Dummett and Eagleton a stage further in a practical direction, by linking it to his own experience of work with the British army in Germany.

E

human activity? One recalls Nkrumah's amiable motto: 'Seek ye first the political kingdom . . .' On the whole, one would have thought Christians would avoid this particular trap, but I can imagine some eager Christian radicals, so intoxicated with the discovery that in battling in the political arena they are doing Christ's work, that they exaggerate the importance of that particular way of doing it. On a basis of respect for persons, one needs to recognise that there are many admirable people in this world, who contribute a great deal to society, but to whom politics means nothing at all. . . .

Political behaviour in a democracy essentially involves compromise and the attainment of some kind of consensus. Individuals or groups may feel disappointed, but they should not feel that they have been treated with savage injustice. The process of compromise has always seemed suspect to reformers, but it has been ably defended by Professor Bernard Crick in his *In Defence of Politics*: compromise is clearly better than the brutal impositions of totalitarian rule, which in effect abolishes political activity.

Nevertheless, there is a considerable element of *impurity* in political behaviour, and I wonder if Catholic radicals who advocate 'political action' are really prepared to accept this. We all know what *pure* activity is: marching and shouting slogans. This can be enormously impressive and very influential in changing public opinion; the Selma march is a memorable example, where the participants showed great physical and moral courage, and went in danger of their lives. There is something unassailable about this kind of purity; but what of the impure but more immediately effective activity of the committee room? Sometimes it is difficult to march; at other times it is rather easy, and would those who took part be equally prepared to participate in the harsh business behind the scenes of politics; to see, for instance, a bill that you passionately believe in trimmed of some of its most important clauses in order to be passed at all? . . .

If Catholic radicals are not going to remain content with the comforts of perpetual opposition, these are issues they will have to face. The freedom of politicians in office to do anything worth while is very much less than it seems in opposition. The contrast between the large promises and claims the Labour Party made before the election, and the painfully modest achievements of the present Government surely makes this clear. (And realising this limitation means, that one should not despise those achievements, inadequate though they are; nothing is easier than the arrogant idealism of those who secretly long for a return to opposition; this is pseudo-politics rather than the real thing.)

There are, admittedly, certainly political questions where all Christians seem agreed; here, one could say, is an absolutely clear moral issue where only one stance is possible. Opposition to Apartheid is an obvious example; it certainly seems so to me. Nevertheless, there is *not* total agreement on this question. Our brothers in Christ of the Dutch Reformed Church firmly believe that Apartheid is defensible in Christians terms (and so, for that matter, does at least one South African Catholic bishop). One can easily say that they are blinded by their history and social and cultural situation; but they could and do say the same thing about us (some very fluent voices have been coming out of Rhodesia and South Africa lately about the way in which the west is 'worm-eaten with liberalism'). The resulting dilemma seems to me this: if we treat the question non-politically it would involve (if the circumstances permitted it) a silencing of these views as pernicious, and this would be a totalitarian solution. Or, one could attempt a dialogue, a debate, an argument; and this would be an attempt at a democratic solution, which is surely preferable. But it would certainly involve Christians quoting scripture at each other in a political argument, which would hardly be edifying. This, again, is something I think one will have to accept if there is to be a full Christian commitment to political life. Moral issues lose some of their sharpness once they are translated into political terms. . . .

It may be objected that I have taken a needlessly low view of politics; nevertheless, the evidence lies all around us, in every issue of the daily paper, that this is what politics means for those involved in it. And yet it is both a necessary and, at times a noble activity. (It might be said that a Christian commitment to politics would purify the means as well as the ends, but this would in effect abolish politics in its essence of reconciling opposed views; one would then have either the Millennium or a terribly efficient totalitarian state.) I am trying not to sound Manichean, since I believe improvement can and does happen; and I would rely on those much-despised worthies, the traditional moral theologians, to exculpate the well-meaning politician from the malice of necessary lying. What I am, I think, saying is that a real commitment to politics means assuming a large part of the imperfection and impurity of the world in order to achieve anything. I realise that I have asked far more questions than I have answered in this article; advisedly for it is more important, first of all, to realise that these questions are implicit in recent Catholic radical discourse, than to try to find answers for them. We often hear that we need a theology of sex; and perhaps there are some signs of the emergence of one. Might I suggest that an even more urgent, and less generally realised, need is for a theology of politics, and even, perhaps, a theology of power?[1]

[1] Bernard Bergonzi, 'What is Politics About?', *New Blackfriars* XLVII, 550 (March 1966), 318–21.

To this Terry Eagleton replied as follows, in April 1966:

'Tell me your definition of politics and I will tell you your politics.' The real breakdown in communication between radical and conservative is about the nature of politics itself, and I find this breakdown acute in reading Bernard Bergonzi's article.

A radical politics summons and activates fundamental belief about the nature of human relationship and tries to sustain this commitment through the detail of actual debate; if it is truly radical, its detailed involvement is controlled by this commitment to an alternative version of man in society. A conservative politics is not convinced that politics is basically about belief; it is itself suspicious of political activity, as inevitably corrupt and crude, intellectually suspect, and rationalises this suspicion by making politics a 'science' or an 'art', a matter of efficiency or running the machine, a dirty but necessary business, or a career like any other. Because it is not gripped by the conviction that politics activates belief, it is liable to be quickly disorientated when it meets other, opposing beliefs; it is driven back on its own bases, hesitant and self-doubting. A conservative politics shows, for reasons that can be argued and understood, the paradox of a deep failure of belief in itself, as anything more than a technique.

Mr Bergonzi seems to me to illustrate most of these points. For him, politics leaves out a good deal of human activity, as his second paragraph makes clear. This, instantly, is the conservative definition: politics as the actual processes of local and national government. The radical's whole effort has been precisely to extend that particular consciousness, to affirm that a radical politics sees art and sexuality, culture and education, language and work, as integral parts of its vision. Again, for Mr

Bergonzi, politics is almost inevitably crude and corrupt: he equates (moral) compromise and the 'attainment of a consensus', as he later links 'lying' and 'manoeuvring'. Radical politics exists to deny that these equations are necessary, while understanding how they can seem inevitable in a particular society, a society where the meaning of politics has been deliberately narrowed, to suit specific interests. To take this as a universal description of what politics is about is to make the mistake of thinking that elections must inevitably involve 'half-truths and monstrous suppressions'. The conservative takes this as unavoidable, part of 'human nature', and begins to shape his politics from there; the radical sees that this particular kind of electioneering, working as it does on formulas of manipulation and 'masses', is part of the reality of the society he opposes, and works for a different politics and a different society.

Finally, the deep hesitation and self-doubt of a conservative politics seems to me there in Mr Bergonzi's puzzling movement between declared political involvement and sudden, serious reservation—reservations which question the whole validity of politics as a human force, as capable of real achievement. The hesitation is there especially in his remarks about South Africa, which seem to me to highlight the conservative and liberal confusion: how can I sustain a belief if this is denied by others? The drive to avoid dogmatism and totalitarianism can become destructive of commitment itself.

I agree that we need a 'theology of politics'; I agree also with Nkrumah's injunction to 'Seek first the political kingdom'. It seems to me that, given the radical definition of politics, this is precisely what Christianity is about.[1]

[1] Terry Eagleton, 'What is Politics About? . . . Terry Eagleton replies to Bernard Bergonzi', *New Blackfriars* XLVII, 551 (April 1966), 372–3.

In August 1966 Donald Nicholl wrote an article in the *Clergy Review* which opened up a different area of discussion. Instead of confining himself to the *definition* of politics, Nicholl criticised the catholic left on a slightly different ground—namely, that its concern with the christian's commitment to political change, combined with the catholic emphasis on the necessity for an organised and visible community in which all christian activity must take place, led at once to the embroilment of the church as such in party politics. The disastrous results of such embroilment had been historically demonstrated, especially in the history of Action Française and similar catholic political movements. It was one of the great gains of the modern era in the church's history to have freed itself from political entanglements of this kind. The catholic left seemed to be advocating a renewed effort to involve the church in politics which, if successful, would lead to a completely catastrophic situation. The thought impressed itself on Nicholl's mind, on his re-reading the works of Action Française writers from the 1920s:

'This stuff is just the sort of stuff that the *Slant* group turns out.' At first I was inclined to dismiss this unbidden thought as totally unlikely—perhaps the polemical tone of the *Action Française* writers had simply reminded me of the unremittingly polemical tone of *Slant* and produced merely a superficial echo of it—after all, it is not on the face of it likely that resemblances will be more than superficial between an extreme Right Wing Neo-Monarchist Movement supported by many Catholics and a Left Wing English Neo-Marxist Catholic group. But then I saw that the resemblance is by no means accidental; it is essential. For both of them believe in the primacy of politics. Indeed, one of the group has lately commended the Nkrumah motto, 'Seek ye first the political kingdom'. Nor is this belief to be wondered at, for in a world dominated by injustice any generous-minded man wishing to change things for the better is inevitably likely to be seduced by the notion that politics has pride of place. How otherwise can we account for *Action Française* attracting such adherents as André Malraux, François Mauriac, Georges Bernanos and Jacques Maritain? And how otherwise account for the mental anguish which some of these people suffered when *Action Française* was condemned? That anguish is nobly recorded for us in Maritain's *Primauté du Spirituel* where we see the scales falling away from the author's eyes and his vision painfully accustoming him to gazing upon the things that are not Caesar's, that do not belong to this world.

This temptation to accord the primacy to politics seems a perennial one. Those early Christians who refused to fall for it were abhorred by loyal citizens of the Roman Empire as 'atheists'; and the Romans were right from their own point of view, because the Christians were refusing to take the political order with total seriousness. The Christians who accepted the Constantinian order had already fallen for the same temptation. So had the extreme papalists in the Middle Ages who defended the temporal power of the papacy. So had Bossuet and the other court preachers of Louis XIV's court who accepted the *roi soleil* on his own terms. So had the supporters of *Action Française*. . . .

Péguy saw at the time of the Dreyfus affair that the Christian *mystique* in France had been perverted into a *politique*; it had virtually become a party rather than the Church: a Right Wing Church is no longer the Church but a party, just as a Left Wing Church is no longer the Church. Péguy saw how easily those who are concerned for public values are constantly in danger of turning a *mystique* into a *politique*, of politicizing life, which means enslaving it by political categories. Whereas the *mystique*, Christianity, should nourish the times spiritually, here the opposite happens; instead of the mystical qualities of tenderness, reverence, magnanimity, etc., humanizing political life on the contrary the political vices of intolerance, fanaticism, power-seeking, etc., de-humanize the Church. To assert the primacy of the political factor means delivering humanity once more to the tyranny of politics from which Christianity had liberated us.[1]

I do not think that the catholic left has yet produced a satisfactory answer to that kind of challenge. But this is hardly surprising. For, once it is granted that the church, in its structural and institutional form as we know it, must never become identified with any particular political orientation, the only answer that can be given is to provide an alternative concept of the church—one that would not be subject to the criticism because it would not be possible for the church, in any case, to think of itself as being an organisation that could compete for allegiance in the political order. In other words, what is required is a theology of the church that does not make it a competitor in politics, while at the same time showing that the individual christian, as a member of the church, must be committed to the left. But more than this is required; for given the possibility of such a concept of the church, it would then be necessary to evolve a practical strategy for turning the idea into concrete reality. In a sense, these two tasks sum up the whole work of the catholic

[1] Donald Nicholl, 'A Layman's Journal', *Clergy Review* LI, 8 (August 1966), 640-2.

left: and it would hardly be fair to dismiss the work done so far on the grounds that these two stupendous problems had not been solved. What should be expected is an awareness, by those who are involved in it, of the nature and size of this undertaking that faces the catholic left. Terry Eagleton's *The New Left Church*, my own *Culture and Liturgy*, and the *Slant Manifesto* (*Catholics and the Left*) all contain some ideas designed to begin the task. But I do not think they can be regarded as more than very tentative steps towards a future that still remains to be properly charted.

A third subject of debate has been the question of the legitimacy or otherwise of revolution as a means for achieving the social changes that the catholic left, in common with the new left itself, demands. A significant contribution to this topic was the *New Black-friars* editorial by Herbert McCabe OP in February 1966. This began by distinguishing two different ways of regarding the liturgical reforms carried out by the bishops since the second Vatican council. If their purpose was to achieve changes in the church smoothly and without fuss, and without a serious danger of creating a split between 'progressives' and 'conservatives', then the English bishops were to be congratulated on the success of their tactics. They were concerned with getting things done, rather than with deliberately manifesting in visible form a new spirit of witness in the church—a spirit that might unduly disturb and worry the traditionalists by its apparent novelty. But *was* 'getting things done' the real need?

It can be argued that the real purpose of the Council was not to reform this or that practice in the Church but to give men a new vision of what the Church is. We may say that if men do not see the Conciliar teaching as new and startling they have not seen it at all. Perhaps the very smoothness and lack of conflict with which the liturgical reforms have been received in England is an indication that they have been presented and accepted as mere tidying up, and not as a revolutionary change. It is possible that many of the clergy and some of the laity would agree with the English Bishop who announced that the Council has changed nothing. If this is so then the cutting edge of the Council has been blunted: what we have beaten into a ploughshare was, perhaps, the sword of the Spirit.

There is a time for doing and a time for saying, a time for bettering the world and a time for martyrdom, for reform and for revolution. The revolutionary and the martyr are impractical men; they are not concerned with improving their world but with witnessing to the possibility of a different world; they seek to say rather than to do. They can always be criticised for wasting an opportunity to help: 'But couldn't you do more good if you *joined* the establishment?' Yet *it is not the man who does good, but the martyr who is, for the Christian tradition, the paradigm case of sanctity.*[1] We are redeemed *not by the cures that Christ did* but by the statement which was his crucifixion.

Some recent Christian thinking seems to forget this. The 'New Morality', for example, makes it a principle to accept the given situation (the given social situation) and do the best we can within its terms; the man whose terms of reference go beyond this situation to the world to come —whether in the Marxist sense or the Christian or both—

[1] The italics in this sentence and throughout the remainder of this quotation are my own, not McCabe's.

is regarded as both impractical and ruthless, one who would sacrifice human happiness to 'abstract' principles. Christian ethics has by now learnt a lot from the liberals and moderates; perhaps the next move in the dialectic is to learn a little from, say, James Baldwin.

Do we want to make it easier for people to live a decent human life within the available inhuman institutions or are we prepared to sacrifice their happiness in order to change the institutions themselves? There is one important strand of Christian tradition according to which all human institutions are more or less equally bad; the change from one set to another can never be worth the cost in human suffering. The only revolution worth dying or inflicting suffering for is the change from this human world to a timeless non-political heaven. Meanwhile the Christian will do his best to ameliorate conditions within whatever happens to be the established order. This we may label the 'conservative' Christian tradition and it has its attendant 'liberalism'. Liberal Christianity is a development of conservatism in which all sets of political institutions are seen as more or less equally good in their time and place (we should seek to understand the headhunters rather than to change them); heaven, however, is eliminated so that we are left with nothing at all that would justify the cost of human suffering—Christianity is seen entirely in terms of being kind to the people you meet. There is, however, a third possibility: that of the Christian who sees the 'permanent revolution' as the counterpart of the 'Ecclesia semper reformanda' (since the Council no longer a 'Protestant' phrase), for whom the coming of the kingdom demands a continual remaking of institutions and of the structures of life and thought. So long as there is tension between doing and saying *there will come times when revolution is the enemy of reform*, when radical change will exact its cost in human suffering, when doing the will of God does not seem to lead to any visible happiness for anybody, when a man is simply a witness to truth and no more. In the meantime it is only in the sacraments that we have a complete unity of saying and doing: 'Efficiat quod figurat', they bring about the new world they proclaim. The sacramental life, which is the Church, is our pledge of the world to come which gives validity to the revolution.[1]

This talk of revolution, and its concomitant concept of martyrdom, provoked Martin Green to a response that eloquently expressed some serious doubts and reservations. In October 1966 he suggested the outlines of an intelligent liberal alternative to the revolutionary commitment of the catholic left.

You describe three kinds of christianity, conservative, liberal, revolutionary, and your descriptions leave the liberal kind much the worst off. Conservative christianity thinks all human institutions equally bad and the only revolution worth the cost is 'the change from this human world to a timeless non-political heaven'. Liberal christianity thinks all institutions equally good, and no revolution worth the human cost; so—since there is no heaven— christianity is only 'being kind to the people you meet'. The revolutionary, *New Blackfriars* christian, of course, sees the *Ecclesia semper reformanda* as the counterpart of the 'permanent revolution'. We must be *permanently* ready for violent change, and today in particular is a time when 'revolution is the enemy of reform, when radical change will exact its cost in human suffering, when doing the will of God does not seem to lead to visible happiness for anybody, when a man is simply a witness to truth and no more.'

[1] Herbert McCabe OP, 'Comment', *New Blackfriars* XLVII, 549 (February 1966), 227–8.

Yes, we must be ready for violence. ready to cause suffering, since we want change. And my agitation at what you say is testimony enough to my own unreadiness, and therefore to its usefulness and necessariness. But I think that agitation testifies also to something else, to some more genuinely reasonable resistance. You exalt the revolutionary particularly at the expense of the liberal. You are asking me, I think, to become attuned to war rather than to peace, to violence, to conspiracy, and to rebellion, rather than to their opposites. And I *know* —using my judgment rather than defending myself—that that choice is a bad one. I mean it is a bad one for us, as Western world intellectuals. Because it involves us in a whole scheme of corrupt and corrupting attitudes . . . to generate and maintain in oneself an exasperated revulsion, a cessation of sympathy, a passionate wish to destroy.

A private world, with private standards, is generated. And within it grows a competition in intensity of the membership feelings—the rejection of the outside world; the intellectual equivalent is the artificial rigour of closed-system logic; and the inevitable result is the heresy hunt.

Nothing is uglier or more destructive than this cosy desperateness. And it seems to me that it must be dishonest, too. For either the desperate man has other kinds of happier experience which he doesn't admit to, which he suppresses intellectually, or else, over ten or twenty years, he must do himself an injury. In the long run, only figures like Genêt and de Sade are pure figures of revolution, saints; in this country it is Dylan Thomas who is called holy in this sense, because he destroyed himself; and your linking of revolutionaries with martyrs gestures in the same direction. Those who are not saints take most of life, though in a capitalist society, pretty much the way other people do. They accept it. This is what I would want them to do, of course. But I would also want them to admit that this is what they are doing, to admit the partiality of their rebellion, to admit that they are liberals as well as revolutionaries; detached as well as involved; individuals as well as members. Without that there comes a conflict between the committed and the uncommitted halves of their lives. Their private happiness takes on the character of a personal indulgence; each half corrupts the other half; look at the protagonists of Doris Lessing's novels. For instance, such people want their children to be happy, and to trust in the world around them, even while they themselves are committed to distrusting it, to being unhappy in it.

That is why we must not become attuned to war rather than peace. We must be attuned to both. We must not hope to hate the society we live in as much as it deserves. The attempt corrupts. Imagine the New York people, having been to see 'Blues for Mr. Charlie', or an underground movie, coming out again on to the hot pavements of New York, seeing everywhere again the works of what they so long ago committed themselves to destroy, going on to a party; what chance have they that the relationships begun or developed there will be anything but destructive?

To be a liberal, to reserve something of oneself, to be incomplete in one's commitment, is not merely to be passive and ineffective. It is to be an adult in ways in which revolutionists are passionate and destructive children. In the day of discussion revolutionists need liberals just as much as in the day of action they need untheoretical soldiers and organizers. From a certain point of view the revolutionist remains an adolescent in relation to both soldier and liberal. That is not the whole truth, of course; we all need to be revolutionists as well as liberals; but it is the half-truth counterpart to your call for us all to become revolutionist *and not* liberals. . . .

I've heard you quote enthusiastically that line from

Graham Greene's new novel, 'I'd rather have blood on my hands than water like Pilate'. I must admit that the liberal, the man who refuses to attune himself to war *and not* to peace, runs the risk of ending up with the water of Pilate on his hands. But I need not, it seems to me, accept the terms of the challenge, especially when it is forced on me under such auspices. Of course Graham Greene sees things that way; of course Waugh did, and Bernanos, and Mauriac; but I thought *New Blackfriars* was offering us some escape from that kind of Catholicism? Surely we aren't still trapped in that underground cellar, conspiring against the world of happiness up there?

To be a revolutionary *and not* a liberal is to hate the world—the world as it now is, as we have known it. And to hate the world is surely wrong. That is the first of my difficulties with the programme you propose.[1]

This response did not satisfy McCabe, however, and the following month he replied in these terms:

As christian revolutionaries the liberalism we oppose is one which by reform would merely conceal the need for more radical change, or one which draws back when the revolutionary consequences of change become clear. . . .

For me there is a place for reform—within the context of revolution. For me there is even a place for violence—with the context of non-violence and forgiveness, the only intrinsically revolutionary act. The programme of christianity is to subvert the world. You object that the revolutionary must 'hate the world—the world as it now is, as we have known it. And to hate the world is surely wrong.' The christian response seems to me more complex: *God so loved the world that he gave his only Son*

[1] Martin Green, 'Comment', *New Blackfriars* XLVIII, 557 (October 1966), 2–5.

. . . not to condemn the world but that the world might be saved through him, but *Do not love the world . . . If any one loves the world, love for the Father is not in him,* and *If you were of the world the world would love its own; but because you are not of the world . . . therefore the world hates you.* The *world* here is not Nature or Creation or Man, it is the actual political and social structures within which christianity is at work. The world's hatred is shown in police actions, in being thrown out of churches, in being stoned or shot down for the sake of law and order by men who think they are doing a service to God.

Christians should be disturbed if their relations with the power-structure are not in some way violent. It is of the nature of the world to dominate by violence and we have not made the world see itself for what it is—we have not 'convinced the world of sin and of righteousness and of judgement'—until we have brought this violence out into the open.

Of course christianity does not offer violence as a solution, it offers crucifixion through which the violent act becomes redemptive. Christianity may also sometimes demand the use of violence but such force only achieves its aim in a context of non-violence. Taken in and by itself it will merely be an expression of destructive hatred.

Violent revolution runs the risk of being mere violence, of being a new attempt at domination and thus of conforming to the world, losing its revolutionary meaning. But this risk must sometimes be taken because the alternative is the certainty of sheer violence and hatred. The alternative to revolution is not always an uneasy peace within which the reformer may work, it is often increasing, though unpublicised, violence. 'I would rather have blood on my hands than the water of Pilate'—the point of this is that Pilate's hands, although he will not see it, are drenched in blood. . . .

There are contexts in which there just is and will be violence and the problem is how to make it redemptive. In a limited and personal case we can do this simply in our hearts by 'offering it up', but outside this narrow field we may have to make of our forgiveness a sign, by suffering persecution for *justice*, and this is a political and a revolutionary act. . . .

Finally to come to your most telling point. 'Imagine the New York people, having been to see "Blues for Mr. Charlie" or an underground movie, coming out again on to the hot pavements of New York, seeing everywhere again the works of what they so long ago committed themselves to destroy, going on to a party; what chance have they that the relationships begun or developed there will be anything but destructive?' Hardly any chance at all; and if the christian church offered no more than a doctrine of protest and a vision of a future ideal, it would fail in human terms as tragically as the communist party. Christians, however, do not just oscillate between protest and parties, each one subtly corrosive of the other. Their fundamental stance is defined by neither of these but by the eucharist, a party, a love-feast whose whole point is a revolutionary act, the crucifixion of Christ. The sacramental life proposes and realises a human relationship which is neither destructive nor conformist but redemptive. That is what the church is for.[1]

The following passage from an article which I wrote for the Council on Religion and International Affairs, and which was published in its journal *Worldview*, may serve to sum up my own feelings with regard to the continuing debate, and point to what seems to me to be the significance of what has been achieved so far:

[1] Herbert McCabe OP, 'Comment', *New Blackfriars* XLVIII, 558 (November 1966), 58–9 and 112.

In order to show the viability of a simultaneous attunement to peace *and* war, it is first of all necessary to show that the determinism that Marxism, and in another sense Burkeian toryism, involve are false analyses of the human situation. It is certainly not enough to speak as though we are quite obviously in a position to choose such a stance, individually, simply by taking thought. Green's use of the word 'attunement' is perhaps deceptive here: for while it suggests (correctly, in my view) that this stance has to consist in achieving a harmony with an objective external state of affairs, it also seems to hint that I can achieve this harmony simply by altering my own personal instrumentality. It's just a matter of my having a good enough ear, and a sufficiently adaptable instrument, to be able to get myself into tune with the rest of the orchestra.

There seem to me to be two conditions necessary to showing the viability of the 'double stance'. The first condition—and this is something rightly insisted upon by the Left, and too little noticed by the liberals—is that the theory, that we are in fact finally determined by external, historical forces, must first of all be decisively refuted. It is not enough, for the Christian at any rate, to say Christianity *affirms* man's freedom, and that therefore it *must* be possible to establish it in the face of all opposition: for the nub of the entire argument is whether Christianity, if this is what it claims, is itself viable or not. What is needed, therefore, is a prolonged, detailed engagement with all the intellectual and historical elements that go to make up this deterministic framework. For example, it is necessary to come to grips with contemporary Marxism in detail, and to understand its case. It has to be shown that what is clearly and obviously valid in it—which, for many of the Catholic Left is at least the main philosophical framework set up in the early works of Marx himself— does not entail that mechanistic determinism which has commonly been attributed to Marxism as its most characteristic historical feature. Some help is offered for this task by modern Marxists themselves; and their work has to be studied and evaluated for this reason. . . .

The second condition—which comes from the liberal side—is that, since the ultimate decision as to when the call to revolution has come is one that only the individual can make, according to his own conscience, it is essential for any *genuine* revolution that the individual should himself be free to determine this moment for himself. And this means that the person who tries to show the viability of the 'double stance' has to prove, against a good deal of historical evidence, that revolution does not necessarily entail the suppression of just that liberty that a personal decision requires. He has, that is to say, to refute (for example) both Orwell and Camus. And this is a task that closed groups are not well equipped to do. For, having proved it to their own satisfaction perhaps, or even (worse still) having put the issue aside for the sake of some ulterior common effort, such groups tend to think the issue is now settled for everyone else. Instead of giving that unremitting, close and sensitive attention to it that it actually requires, if the revolution is to get beyond remaining a minority cult within a majority indifference, they tend to bypass or underestimate it.

McCabe admits, significantly, that Christianity affirms that these two conditions can be fulfilled. That is to say, it affirms that the coming Kingdom will truly be a society in which peace and war, liberal *and* revolutionary values, have come together in a new coalescence, and also that in some sense—perhaps undiscernible, but real—history is moving towards that consummation. But this affirmation is rather like the belief that it is possible to arrive at the concept of God with certainty by the use of reason alone. We acknowledge, notionally, that the trick can be done; but we don't for the life of us see how. And perhaps the chief value of the current debate is that it is forcing people to see that it is dishonest to rest here. We have to give it the unremitting attention and effort that it continually requires. The significance of the Catholic Left is that, by drawing attention to the revolutionary aspect of the double stance—an aspect scandalously neglected, not only in the immediate past but also in the most up-to-date reforming circles of the Church—it has helped to make this effort possible. Whether it will succeed, or even whether it *can* succeed, I do not pretend to know. All I do know is that it is the most important task facing Western Christianity at the present time, and that the Left is to be thanked for having understood this and tried to do something about it.[1]

[1] Brian Wicker, 'The Catholic Left in Britain', *Worldview* (November 1966), 4–7.

Bibliography

Articles and contributors to collections cited

ALTHUSSER, Louis, 'Contradiction and Over-determination', *New Left Review* 41 (January–February 1967), 15–35.

ANDERSON, Perry, 'The Left in the Fifties', *New Left Review* 29 (January–February 1965), 14–15.

ANDERSON, Perry, 'Problems of Socialist Strategy', *Towards Socialism*, ed. P. Anderson and R. Blackburn, London, Fontana (1965), 221–90.

BERGER, Peter, and Stanley Pullberg, 'Reification and the Sociological Critique of Consciousness', *New Left Review* 35 (January–February 1966), 57.

BERGONZI, Bernard, 'What is Politics About?' *New Blackfriars* LXVII, 550 (March 1966), 318–21.

BOXER, Charles, OP, 'The church as a community in the world: 1. A parish experience', *Slant* 13 (February–March 1967), 3–10.

BOXER, Charles, OP, 'The church as a community in the world: 2. An interpretation', *Slant* 14 (April–May 1967), 21–4.

CLEGG, Ian, 'Self-management in Yugoslavia', *Slant* 13 (February–March 1967), 13–17.

CLEGG, Ian, 'Workers' control: a short history', *Slant* 11 (October–November 1966), 3–6.

CLEGG, Ian, 'Workers' self-management in Algeria', *Slant* 12 (December 1966–January 1967), 16–19.

COOPER, David, 'Two Types of Rationality', *New Left Review* 29 (January–February 1965), 62–8.

COOPER, David, 'Violence in Psychiatry', *Views* 8 (Summer 1965), 18–24.

CUNNINGHAM, Adrian, and Terry Eagleton, 'Politics', *Catholics and the Left* ('Slant Manifesto'), London, Sheed & Ward (1966), 4–5.

DUMMETT, Michael, 'How Corrupt is the Church?' *New Blackfriars* XLVI, 542 (August 1965), 619–28; reprinted in *The Purification of the Church*: five comments from *New Blackfriars*, ed. Ian Hislop OP (London 1967), 27–39.

DUMMETT, Michael, 'Church and World: Mr Dummett Replies', *New Blackfriars* XLVII, 546 (December 1965), 139–40.

EAGLETON, Terry, 'The Language of Renewal', *New Blackfriars* LXVII, 544 (October 1965), 21–3.

EAGLETON, Terry, 'What is Politics About? Terry Eagleton replies to Bernard Bergonzi', *New Blackfriars* LXVII, 551 (April 1966), 372–3.

FLEET, Ken, 'Workers' Control: the movement in Britain', *Slant* 11 (October–November 1966), 6–8.

GREEN, Martin, 'Comment', *New Blackfriars* LXVIII, 557 (October 1966), 2–5.

LASH, Nicholas, 'The Eucharist: Sacrament of Christ's Presence in the World', *New Blackfriars* XLVIII, 560 (January 1967), 172–85.

McCABE, Herbert, OP, 'Comment', *New Blackfriars* LXVII, 549 (February 1966), 227–8.

McCABE, Herbert, OP, 'Comment', *New Blackfriars* XLVIII, 558 (November 1966), 58–9 and 112.

McCABE, Herbert, OP, 'Comment', *New Blackfriars* XLVIII, 561 (February 1967), 227–8.

NICHOLL, Donald, 'A Layman's Journal', *Clergy Review* LI, 8 (August 1966), 640–2.

REDFERN, Martin, 'The church, sacrament of a socialist society', *Catholics and the Left* ('Slant Manifesto'), London, Sheed & Ward (1966), 148–82.

STEIN, Walter, 'Humanism and Tragic Redemption', *New Blackfriars* LXVIII, 561 (February 1967), 230–44.

STEIN, Walter, 'Redemption and Revolution', *New Blackfriars* LXVIII, 562 (March 1967), 319–26.

STEIN, Walter, 'Redemption and Tragic Transcendence', *Slant* 15 (June/July 1967), 3–10.

WICKER, Brian, 'The Catholic Left in Britain', *Worldview* (November 1966), 4–7.

WICKER, Brian, 'The Future of Belief', *New Blackfriars* LXVIII, 565 (June 1967), 468–78.

WICKER, Brian, 'Liturgy and Politics', *New Blackfriars* XLVII, 551 (April 1966).

WICKER, Brian, 'The Ministry of the Word', *New Blackfriars* XLVII, 545 (November 1965), 61–7.

WICKER, Brian, 'Theology and the New Left', *Slant* 1 (Spring 1964), 8–14.

WILLIAMS, Raymond, 'New Left Catholics', *New Blackfriars* XLVIII, 558 (November 1966), 75.

Suggested Further Reading

AMERY, Carl, *Capitulation: an Analysis of Contemporary Catholicism*, London, Sheed & Ward (1967).

BROTHERS, Joan, *Church and School*, Liverpool University Press (1964).

CAMERON, J. M., *The Night Battle*, London, Burns & Oates (1962), 1–17, 50–75.

CONRAD, Joseph, *Lord Jim* (1900).

DEWART, Leslie, *Cuba, Church and Crisis*, London, Sheed & Ward (1964).

DEWART, Leslie, *The Future of Belief*, London, Burns & Oates (1967).

EAGLETON, Terry, *The New Left Church*, London, Sheed & Ward (1966).

HALLORAN, James D., *Control or Consent? A Study of the Challenge of Mass Communications*, London, Sheed & Ward (1963).

HOGGART, Richard, *Uses of Literacy*, London, Chatto & Windus (1957); and Harmondsworth, Penguin (1958).

LAING, R. D., *The Divided Self*, London, Tavistock Publications (1959); and Harmondsworth, Penguin (1965).

LAING, R. D., *The Self and Others*, London, Tavistock Publications (1961).

LAING, R. D., and D. Cooper, *Reason and Violence*, London, Tavistock Publications (1964).

LAING, R. D., and A. Esterson, *Sanity, Madness and the Family*, London, Tavistock Publications (1964).

LAWLOR, Monica, *Out of this World*, London, Sheed & Ward (1965).

MIDDLETON, Neil, and others, *Catholics and the Left* ('Slant Manifesto'), London, Sheed & Ward (1966).

ORWELL, George, 'Politics and the English Language', *Collected Essays*, London, Secker & Warburg (1961), 359.

ROBINSON, J. A. T., *The Body*, London, SCM Press (1952).

STEIN, Walter (ed.), *Nuclear Weapons and Christian Conscience*, London, Morton Press (1961).

STEIN, Walter (ed.), *Peace on Earth: the Way Ahead*, London, Sheed and Ward (1966).

TIDMARSH, Mannes, OP, James D. Halloran, and K. J. Connolly, *Capital Punishment: a Case for Abolition*, London, Sheed & Ward (1963).

WICKER, Brian, *Culture and Liturgy*, London, Sheed & Ward, (1963).

WICKER, Brian, *Culture and Theology*, London, Sheed & Ward (1966).

WILLIAMS, Raymond, *Modern Tragedy*, London, Chatto & Windus (1966).

WILLIAMS, Raymond, *The Long Revolution*, London, Chatto & Windus (1961); and Harmondsworth, Penguin (1965).

WINDASS, Stanley, *Christianity versus Violence: a Social and Historical Study of War and Christianity*, London, Sheed & Ward (1964).

WITTGENSTEIN, Ludwig, *Philosophical Investigations*, Oxford, Blackwell (1958²).

WITTGENSTEIN, Ludwig, *Tractatus Logico-Philosophicus*, London, Routledge (1922).

ZAHN, Gordon, *German Catholics and Hitler's War*, London, Sheed & Ward (1963).

Index